Dedicated to Ruby

Contents

My name is Ruben Romero; I've worked in the marketing and professional content creation industry for over 18 years. I've created tons of content even before it was the popular thing to do online: Pre-Facebook, Pre-YouTube, even Pre-Myspace.

I've held different positions in this industry such as graphic designer, web designer, media & marketing director, studio manager, creative director, magazine editor, lead photographer/videographer, and TV show producer.

I've had the privilege of working with major companies such as GUESS, top law firms, attorneys, plastic surgeons, doctors, and dozens of major celebrities. I have been featured in FOX, CBS, NBC, INFLUENCIVE, and NY Weekly. My work has been seen on several billboards, and even on a NY Times Square billboard for GUESS.

Today, I am known more for being the founder of Stunner Studios (a highly recognized photo, video, and podcast studio) in Houston, TX, and Alpha Magazines' magazine editor. I've been called a one-man media and marketing army, and some have referred to me as a "Marketing Da Vinci."

I believe if done right, marketing is an art form, just like creating quality content. Creating something out of nothing, delivering it to the right audience, while approaching it from an artistic perspective is something I've mastered over the years.

The issue is that creating content is only half the battle. It's knowing how, where, and in what way to distribute that content that makes you successful. Times have changed drastically in the last decade when it comes to marketing and creating content.

Nowadays, making just a few pieces of content a week won't cut it anymore. Brands are pumping out hundreds of pieces of content a month or even in a week! That's right, you read correctly! Creating hundreds of pieces of content a month is now the new norm. Things are not slowing down, either.

I get asked questions every day about some of the things I've been able to accomplish. So, In this book, I would like to share with you some of the things that made me and the businesses I've worked with successful. I will also share with you what you can expect to see in marketing trends going forward.

01: User Generated Content (UGC)

"The Modern Day DaVinci"

What's the Definition?

Social media influencers create and share large amounts of user-generated content for brands, destinations, and businesses. User-generated content can influence shoppers by using followers as billboards, using their social feeds as digital shop windows for shopping, or listening to their followers.

User-generated content is a valuable asset in social media marketing and has an incomparable authenticity, that shows a real appreciation for your brand. It is an ideal scenario for marketers when they help a brand generate highly creative pieces of content for campaigns. The first step is to select a form of content to create and formulate catchy hashtags. Starting with original UGC that can be distributed on all online platforms is the ideal scenario, and the second is the strategy of how to distribute your content.

This is good news for brands. They can use the brand hashtags to spread user-generated content across social media while regularly sharing their best contributions with content creators with appropriate recognition. This is the first step towards creating a UGC hashtag campaign and paves the way for its successful introduction on social media. For B2B brands, there are several different types of user-generating content campaigns available – think reviews of supplied products or referral videos!

Social media marketers can learn a lot by watching user-generated content, such as memes that come from the same users you want to address, which gives you a better understanding of their feelings about your brand. User-generated content helps you gain insight into the audience, improving your marketing campaign and making it more robust. It is particularly popular when combined with other types of content such as social media posts, videos, photos, and memes.

When you share content generated by social media users, make sure you pay clear tribute to the original creator. That's the clear-cut rule of sharing, but otherwise, the user is helping to make the marketing effort for you!

A Bit More Depth Than That…

As you've already guessed, there's a little more to this idea! Let's delve a bit further.

Effective Social Media Strategies

Any good business owner or marketer will know that to be successful with a social media account in business, it's vital to have the right strategies to gain attention from the maximum amounts of people at the right times. When it comes to social media video marketing, it is vital to have good marketing strategies to ensure that you get the best results. For example, the timing of your videos is key to getting a good response.

Some of the best times to post videos on your social media pages are during lunchtime and in the evenings, when most people are not working and are more likely to relax and catch up on social media. Similarly, the weekends are also a good time to increase your video-sharing activity.

However, bear in mind that timing could vary depending on your specific target audience, so it's essential to ensure that you carry out the necessary market research before putting this strategy in place. For example, if you're targeting students, you may get a better response by posting late at night or in the mid-morning.

On the other hand, businesses targeting people who work in typical 9-5 jobs are best sticking to evenings and weekends to update their social media pages with fresh new video content.

Generating Interest in Social Media

To generate interest in your video content on social media, it's important to make sure that you use other content forms to grab your followers' attention. While some social media sites, such as Instagram, may play your video content automatically, others, such as Facebook, may require the user to actively press the play button to view the video. In this case, using written content to create an interesting and attention-grabbing description of the video will encourage more users to press play.

When it comes to writing good video descriptions on social media, it's important to remember to keep things short. To the point – anything too long could end up boring the reader, and they might not bother to watch the video after reading. A good way to create interesting and compelling video descriptions is to leave the reader wondering. For example, a simple 'Can you guess what happened when we went here?' will leave the user wanting to find out more, encouraging them to take the time to watch the video.

Growing Your Social Media Presence Through Video

Video is one of the best types of content for increasing your social media presence and gaining more followers. Since video is available on the main social media networks – Facebook, Twitter, Instagram, and Snapchat – it's easy for businesses to upload their videos to YouTube and share them on the various social media platforms to reach a broader audience.

We have already seen the power of social media and video combined – more and more people are rising to internet fame through short, humorous, or informative videos on social media than ever before. Businesses such as make-up and cosmetics stores and artists are using social media to grow their businesses through short tutorial videos.

Similarly, food bloggers are utilizing video to its full extent by creating short, catchy recipe videos, which are extremely popular. The key to using video to grow your business' presence on social media is to create shareable content and actively ask your followers to share it.

When creating video content, it's a good idea to study your target audience and find out what they enjoy sharing with their personal social media followers. When you create content that your direct followers love to share, you will expose it to a much wider audience.

Video – A Grand Connection Tool

Using video to connect with your social media followers is becoming more and more popular for businesses and has many great benefits. As mentioned earlier, social media and the online shopping boom mean that customer service is now something that is expected 24/7. Customers expect to be kept up to date with their favorite brands through social media networks such as Facebook, Twitter, Instagram, YouTube, and Snapchat.

Facebook Live Video

One of the best ways to keep your customers up to date using social media and video is Facebook's Live Video feature. Not only does Facebook now allow you to keep your customers up to date in real-time when you're doing something special such as attending a big industry event, taking part in charity fundraising, or unveiling a big new product, it also allows you to communicate directly with your customers, for example through live question and answer sessions. When you stream a live video on Facebook, you can see the comments being left on it. This means that you can ask your followers to leave any questions in the comments, where you can read them and answer straight away as the asker watches. This can be a great tool to use when it comes to finding out what customers want to know about your business or what they would like to see in the way of changes and adjustments.

Snapchat

Snapchat was once exclusively for teens and young people. Still, today, more and more businesses understand the power of this app when it comes to connecting with customers. With more and more people of all ages signing up to Snapchat every day, having a brand Snapchat account can be a great way to communicate with your customers and get more exposure for your brand. Although Snapchat videos only last a matter of seconds, short, to-the-point videos can be hugely effective, or you can use a sequence of short videos to tell a story or share what you are currently doing with your followers.

Foundational Stones

To create a personal branding strategy that will be successful and add value to your venture, you first need to begin with a solid foundation.

Much like with a house, if there are cracks in the foundation, it will not be long before the whole thing crumbles.

While setting out and clearly defining your brand may feel like it takes a lot of time to do—it is an upfront time investment. Once everything is visibly developed and strategized, it will make the remainder of the business planning a breeze.

However, it is also important to note that you should also be monitoring your branding strategy as your business unfolds.

Monitoring should be a part of your admin—over time; it will become second nature. There will be more on this later, but first, let us utilize three questions to determine your brand's baseline.

As we go on, it is essential to remember that everything needs to be very clearly defined—if you are confused about your branding, your audience will be, too.

What is your purpose?

This is a very abstract and confronting question. It is prudent to note that this phase of developing your branding strategy will require some deep reflection and reflective thinking. While it is intense, you will know yourself and what you want your dream life to look like.

You need to understand yourself, including your motivations and personality, to harness the best elements to shine in your branding.

Multiple things need to be considered, and different people value them in different ways. You need to decide the most important and most relevant attributes to be manipulated into your branding. It can be helpful to make a list of the following.

-Past successes?

-Strengths?

-Goals?

-Experiences?

-Passions?

-Personality traits?

-Values?

-Beliefs?

-Interests?

What are the words that you want to be used in and associated with your brand? Write down as many things as you can think of for each of the categories above. Then go through and highlight the ones that stand out to you. They should be the most important and most usable ones that can inspire your branding.

Do not be afraid to use your life! Your experiences, strengths, and ambitions are what make you, you. They are what will make your audience connect with you.

Who Is Your Audience?

Now that you have figured out a little more about who you are, you need to select your target audience. Defining your target audience means that you can tailor your content and marketing specifically and efficiently towards them.

It can be helpful to come up with a very specific image of a consumer.

First, what is the main demographic of your target audience?

-Age

-Location

-Gender

-Lifestyle

-Education

-Financial situation

-The tech they use

-Living situation

-Family situation

Then, you need to think about them more psychologically.

-What do they want?

-What do they need?

-What challenges do they face?

-What do they believe in?

-What are their attitudes and behaviors?

Defining your target audience as specifically as possible is a great
way to ensure that your branding can be optimized for your potential

future customers.

You need to make sure that the words you have chosen for your branding will also resonate and reflect well on your audience—otherwise, it leads to mixed signals and suboptimal performance.

What do you have to offer?

Based on your purpose and your audience, what can you do for them?

Why is it better than everything else on the market?

-Making their life easier?

-It is solving a problem that they have?

-It is solving a problem that they do not know that they have?

-Making their life more interesting or entertaining?

-Are you helping them?

-Teaching them something?

Knowing Your Math

Now that you have decided on your target audience, the platforms you will be using to share it, and its content, will be essential in tracking its progress.

Analytics can be confusing to understand initially, but once you are familiar with them and how they benefit you, they will allow you to fine-tune your content to post and maximize your branding returns.

Checking your analytics allows you to monitor, reflect, and recreate your personal branding's success—and may help you catch any shortcomings early on.

Intense growth does not always happen overnight, and it can be unrealistic to go viral immediately. But, by tracking your progress, you can capitalize on your personal branding's successes as they happen.

Are You Undergoing Complete Engagement?

Engagement is a two-way street. The first form of engagement is audience engagement. Engagement occurs not when your audience views your post, but when they like it, commenting on it, sharing it, and taking action from it.

Most platforms have built-in insights and engagement checking functionality.

You can see the demographic breakdown of your followers (to make sure you are reaching your target audience), as well as the number of likes. One of the most important forms of engagement is the number of people who have seen the most versus the number of people who have taken action from it (including likes, shares, and comments). If you have many viewers, but low actions are taken, this could mean that your content is not resonating with your audience.

Alternatively, if your posts are not being seen, consider changing your content schedule. Ensure you are posting when your audience is active and include a call to action in your content.

The other form of important engagement is your own. Are you regularly checking your accounts, responding to comments, replying to questions, or just otherwise interacting with your audience?

This makes your branding accessible, credible, and authentic. You want your audience to feel like they can trust you, and if you are online, you are available.

Putting Keyword Planning and Search Engine Optimization to Work
Search engine optimization and keyword planning, in essence, just make you more easily found when audiences search for relevant things to your brand.

Planning out keywords is a good step to take when trying to reach your audience. Use words relevant to your branding and industry, making sure you check for popular words and phrases.

The popular and common searches do change over time, so ensure that you keep up with the trends. Audiences also change their word searches depending on the satisfaction with the results—so try and keep synonyms in mind.

Search engines rank search results, and the higher up in the results you are, the more credible and more trustworthy you will seem. How many times do you go to the second page of results?

Tailoring your branding to be optimized for search engines is a perfect way to show your audience that you are credible. Search engine optimization is an organic way of gaining traffic to your profiles and naturally growing an audience.

Get Younger Customers by Using Snapchat (That's User-Generated Video!)

With the younger generation having the highest number of people who are more likely to choose to shop online over any other age group, it's no surprise that businesses are increasingly targeting those between the ages of 16-30. Online sales are beginning to make up a bigger portion of most businesses' total profits, with more and more companies in existence that operate solely on the web. To increase sales, businesses are using social media to reach out to the younger generation, who are often more likely to buy products online due to social media advertisements and updates.

Why Snapchat Works

Snapchat has become more and more popular since its beginnings just a few years ago. Starting off as a photo-sharing app where the photo is deleted after the number of seconds specified by the sender, Snapchat now has a range of features such as the 'My Story' option, Snapchat chat, and the option to send videos and photographs both directly from the Snapchat app and from the user's camera roll. Several big businesses have also taken to Snapchat. It is regularly used to update users and give them the inside scoop on different events worldwide, such as the Olympic Games, Fashion Week, or the Oscars. Businesses can use Snapchat to update their followers on what they are doing, making it a powerful tool for being a relatable brand that feels more of a 'friend' than a business. Other Snapchat features can also be utilized to better connect with your customers; for example, you could ask followers to send in their snaps using your products, which you will replay to a bigger audience. This not only improves your relationship with your customers and helps them to feel valued and more involved in your company, but it's also a great advertisement for you!

Why Businesses Need Snapchat

Suppose you're already using the main social media networks – Facebook, Twitter, and perhaps Instagram – to upload videos and other types of content for your users to see. In that case, you might be wondering if there's much point in getting Snapchat for your business. Even though Snapchat may not yet be seen as one of the main social networks, it is growing rapidly and has a lot of potential to be massive in the future. More and more people are choosing to use Snapchat over other social media options to connect with their friends and family since it is more 'to the point' than many other social media networks and provides users with a simple but effective way to stay in touch with not only their personal friends but also with the brands that they love. Setting up a Snapchat account that your customers and potential customers can follow is a great way to help them feel that they are more connected to your brand. You'll earn even more customer relations points if you allow people to send you snaps or even follow users back!

What Can You Share On Snapchat?

The beauty of Snapchat is that it can be used to share a whole range of different things. You can upload photographs of your latest products, store openings, the office, or anything else in your business that you think your target audience will be interested in seeing. Taking videos of the different things going on inside your business will give your audience an insider's look and help them to better connect with your brand. Being able to connect with a brand today is an important factor for many consumers when looking to purchase products and services, especially within the younger generation, with many young consumers purchasing products simply because they feel a connection with that brand, even if there are better products available from competing brands.

Using Snapchat for Research

Snapchat is also a great tool for research when it comes to understanding your target audience and learning more about their preferences, likes, and dislikes. When you connect with your customers on Snapchat, you can find out about them in many different ways. For example, you may be able to follow them to watch what they upload to Snapchat, or ask your

followers to send in Snaps and chats answering different questions which you will ask. Holding a 'Q&A' session on Snapchat, which you'll advertise beforehand not only on the app but also on a range of other platforms, can be a very effective way to gain more Snapchat followers, get your followers to share your content, and find out more about your target audience and get to know what they want. Not only does this improve your knowledge of your target audience, but it also has a lot of potential to provide you with a range of other benefits such as increasing your online presence, improving profits, and boosting customer satisfaction.

Why So Popular?

Business owners who keep pace with marketing trends will know that video marketing is huge. As more social networks adapt to Facebook's "live" feature, which allows corporate and personal account holders to include live video feeds recorded on their smartphones in their timelines, it is time for small business owners to embrace this new trend that ensures they are not left behind.

Video content is a hugely powerful way to get your message out. Many different types of video content could be used for business marketing purposes. There is marketing content where you create a short film that convinces a customer to show interest in your brand.

Some marketing videos focus on your brand as a whole, while others focus on a particular product or service. Some marketing videos focus on a particular product, such as an advertising campaign or marketing campaign for a brand's products or services. In contrast, others focus on specific products and services.

Another type of marketing video that you may encounter when using video content is a video product review. You can use actors, animations, or something else to compile your marketing videos. Still, the most common use case for video reviews and product reviews is currently being reviewed.

Product reviews are hugely important, as many people rely on other people's reviews when buying products and services online. However, video product reviews do not have a written rating. They can be very effective, so the best way to get them is to send a sample product to an industry vlogger or video blogger and ask him to submit a video review. There are also cases where you could use an app like Snapchat to allow users to post small videos.

What type of video content you can use depends on you, but whether it's a product description, a video review, or even a blog post about the product in general.

This gives customers a clear idea of the product and allows them to make a more informed purchase decision. As online shopping becomes more popular, competition for an online business increases as more people open their laptops instead of taking to the streets. This has led to online retailers looking for new and innovative ways to generate interest in their products online, which leads to more sales. This is especially useful for many people who want to see their products in person before buying, such as clothing, shoes, accessories, and other things in a store.

Whether your business is online or not, it is absolutely essential to have an online presence, whether through social media such as Facebook, Twitter, Instagram, Pinterest, YouTube, or other platforms. Suppose you own a company that does not sell products online. In that case, it can be effective to upload videos describing your products to platforms like YouTube before sharing them on your social media pages to generate more interest and boost sales. As videos become more accessible, even small businesses on a small budget can share video content on their Snapchat or Facebook pages. Any company that has an online presence should use video content in one form or another.

As video content becomes increasingly popular to connect with customers online, the market is becoming more demanding. Today's customers increasingly expect their favorite companies and brands to allow them to watch and rewatch video content, whether on social media such as Facebook, Twitter, Instagram, Pinterest, YouTube, or other platforms. As online video platforms such as YouTube, Snapchat, Facebook, and Instagram become more popular, today's consumers expect to connect with brands they are associated with through video content.

Today's customers are not only looking for products and services that meet their current needs, but it is becoming increasingly important for them to connect with the brands they buy from and connect with. Customers will judge brands by the products or services they search for and buy, not by the way they present themselves on social media. This is why video content offers companies of all sizes the opportunity to improve customer satisfaction, and satisfy their existing and potential customers.

Using Video for Describing and Reviewing Your Products

Every video platform, including YouTube, Facebook, Instagram, and Snapchat, provides you with a great opportunity to upload video product descriptions and reviews. For many businesses, YouTube is a natural choice for creating and uploading video product descriptions and reviews. It can be viewed both on YouTube itself and shared on a whole range of other platforms, including Facebook, Twitter, and even embedded on blogs and websites. YouTube's huge shareability means that you will be able to reach a wider audience with your video product descriptions and reviews. Since people are more likely to share videos than any other type of content, and YouTube allows them to share it on a wide range of different platforms, it makes your content available to an even wider audience and creates genuine backlinks to your site and YouTube channel which therefore improves your business' SEO.

Video product descriptions are becoming a hugely effective tool for marketing online. Not only can video descriptions be used for providing potential customers with a first-hand view of the products that you sell on your website, but they can also be used for marketing purposes by uploading them onto social media websites, where people who are not familiar with your brand may find them and become interested. There are many different benefits of using video product descriptions. The main one is that they are more engaging for your customers. When you provide your customers with a video product description instead of text and photographs, it allows them to get a first-hand look at the product and what it looks like in real life when used. For some products, a video description could be made in the form of a how-to guide, which shows the customer how to use it to get the best results from it once they've purchased it. Another example would be clothing stores, which could provide a catwalk video of their fashion pieces in action. Video product descriptions can also affect making customers relate to the product more as they watch others use it in the types of ways they would.

Don't Ignore Instagram!

Suppose you've kept up with the development of Instagram. In that case, you'll know that the photo-sharing app is fast becoming one of the most popular social media platforms in the world. In the past, Instagram may have gained a reputation as a boring photo-sharing app. Today's modern consumer is a very busy person and does not want to waste time watching lengthy videos, especially when there is a quicker way to get your message out. Short, pointed videos have proved to be a highly effective marketing tool, even though Instagram only allows users to upload minute-long videos.

One of the best examples of an Instagram video is a makeup artist. It's a great example of how Instagram works in the world of makeup.

Professional Mua Beauty bloggers quickly realize the benefits when they use Instagram videos for marketing. They make short and sweet tutorials that are speeded up to fit into Instagram's short timeframe, and hardworking users get the latest video updates from their favorite brands. For example, a make-up enthusiast can scroll through Instagram to learn how to get her latest look from her favorite brand in less than ten minutes. It will be a huge hit with her followers, who will learn how to wear a look that lasts 45 minutes without having to watch a video that has lasted so long.

Some of the most popular videos on Instagram are usually about telling a story or showing a series of steps on doing something.

Depending on the type of company you run, you can include these videos in your Instagram feed. For example, how videos about the products you sell can help get your followers' attention and great advertising methods to help you get more attention to your product. Use Instagram videos to connect better with your customers. When it comes to the brand you're engaging with, upload your video to Instagram as soon as possible. While some videos need to be speeded up to ensure they fit into Instagram's timeframe, this can provide users with a quick way to stay up to date and learn something new.

Browsing through things that inspire your followers on Instagram can help you get a better picture of your target audience and determine what you should post to get their attention and interest. Although some followers have private Instagram accounts, many of them post their uploads publicly.

One of the best things about Instagram is using links to your videos and photo descriptions. This means that it generates more interest in your content and more attention so that viewers wonder what else happened after they saw the preview. For this reason, it works well as a sharing platform. Suppose you upload a video or interview with a celebrity to your site. In that case, you can use Instagram to promote the clip by uploading a link to a movie that users can watch along with the movie.

Reaching Out to Customers Through Video Descriptions

Businesses quickly realize the power of video product descriptions when reaching out to their customers and generating more interest in their brand. Not only does a video product description double up as a great marketing tool that can be shared on various social media and video platforms, but it can also be used in such a way that the customer feels a stronger connection to the brand and product. For example, a toy store targeting young children's parents could use a video product description that features toddlers having fun and playing with the toy. This is much more likely to resonate with a parent, who will find it easier to visualize their own child enjoying the product that they're viewing.

Why Video Product Reviews Are So Effective

When it comes to using video to advertise, market, and promote your products, video product reviews can be hugely effective. Product reviews are already an important part of shopping online, with a huge range of sites dedicated to reviewing various businesses and establishments. Bloggers regularly profit from testing and reviewing the products from different businesses and brands in their industry, whether via written content or video.

Video bloggers, known as vloggers, have become more and more popular in recent times. Vloggers cover a whole range of different topics, whether they're traveling around the world in their videos, creating beauty tutorials, gaming, cooking, and baking, DIY, following their pets, or even creating funny prank and parody videos. The reality is, vloggers can be hugely popular people online, with many making a name for themselves simply because the videos that they post generate a lot of attention. When it comes to reaching out to a wider audience, vloggers are people who are in a great position to help you out. Finding a vlogger who has a large following and creating videos related to your business' industry is a great way to get the word out there by creating a video product review. Depending on the type of products you want them to review, you may be able to review their vlog in return for sending them a product to test free of charge. In contrast, others may accept payment for advertising your brand in their videos.

Video Reviews: The Personal Touch

Anyone who is considering making a serious, important, or expensive purchase online without testing out the product first will prioritize reading customer reviews. Any good e-commerce site knows that allowing customers to leave reviews for the business as a whole and for each specific product can go a long way to building trust with customers and improving customer relations. However, although reading written reviews can provide your customers with a lot of information about a product to make an informed decision about purchasing it, a video review can have a 'personal' touch that resonates stronger. Actually, watching and listening to a person review a product can have a much bigger impact on a customer than simply reading about it. When somebody is watching another person reviewing a product, they benefit from seeing things such as facial expressions and body language, which can tell the viewer a lot. This is often missed in written product reviews, where it can often be easy to misunderstand things.

Using Video Reviews to Connect with Your Customers

The great thing about video today is that anybody can make a video in a matter of minutes or even seconds. Modern smartphones all have great video-shooting capabilities and features, so not only is it easier for businesses of all sizes to shoot and upload videos to their social media sites, but their customers can also do it too! There are many different ways to use video to connect with and communicate better with your customers. Asking them to leave video reviews of your products that they've purchased from you is an effective and fun way to do this. Holding a competition for the best video where the winner gets a prize, for example, is a good way to generate interest in your company, boost sales, and improve customer satisfaction. Not only does asking customers to send in their own video product reviews allow them to engage with your brand, but it also encourages them to buy from your brand to do a product review and share the competition with their friends and followers. By asking customers to create video product reviews, you can expose your brand and products to a larger audience when they upload and share their videos to their own social media profiles. Video reviews could be uploaded on YouTube, Facebook, Instagram, Snapchat, or all of them!

Don't Forget YouTube!

YouTube, the world's largest video platform, has become the go-to platform on which you can watch videos of literally everything. Video is a relatively new trend in social media. YouTube is the only video platform that has existed for years. While it was possible to share videos on Facebook and Twitter in the early days, the ability to tag you by creating a video profile was only introduced a few years ago.

With millions of users who like to spend their free time looking for new and interesting videos, it makes sense for companies of all sizes to have their own YouTube channel.

When it comes to marketing your brand and products through videos, YouTube is the first place you can turn when it comes to it. With WordPress, you can integrate the latest YouTube video uploads directly into your blog. You can upload YouTube videos to your business blog by copying and pasting the links into the HTML of your blogs. Use the videos you upload to YouTube to share with your customers, employees, and other business community members.

Having a YouTube channel that is regularly updated with fresh and interesting content that attracts the attention of your target audience can be hugely beneficial for SEO. You can also take the opportunity to create genuine and authentic backlinks on your business website or blog. Including keywords such as company name and location in YouTube videos or product descriptions can also improve your search engine rankings in general and local Google search results. The words you choose when creating an informative video description mean you can insert important keyword phrases.

By uploading your own videos to YouTube, you can use the popular marketing platform to further promote your brand, products, and services. Many official YouTube users upload short commercials that can be shown in your videos. YouTube is also a great resource for industries that regularly post updates and have several followers.

One of the best things about YouTube is that it's easy to use and fun, especially when connecting with your audience. You can allow your viewers to comment on your videos. By allowing them to comment, you'll get an insight into which videos are popular and which are not. Actively asking your customers to leave their opinions and views on YouTube videos is a great way to show them that you value them and that their voice matters to you. This means that you feel valued by your brand. It can also help you improve customer loyalty, which is key to building a good connection and relationship between you and your audience.

With so many brands jumping on YouTube channels, the secret to success when using the video platform is to always be something different and unique in what you do. Of course, you want to use your YouTube channel to showcase your products, services, and anything else you want to share with your viewers. Still, you need to get really creative when uploading videos to your brand's YouTube channel. Keeping up with what the competition on Google + and YouTube are doing is key to ensuring you're not left behind.

Don't Be Afraid to Request Those Shares!

Studies have shown that users who request shares are more likely to get them than those who do not. And last but not least, there are several ways to promote the active sharing of videos on social media such as Facebook, Twitter, YouTube, and Instagram.

Actively asking for shares at the end of your video or in the video description can prompt your followers to click the Share button. After all, it only takes a second. A good number of parts can be crucial to increase your audience's reach for your content when you upload your videos to video platforms and social media sites.

One of the best ways to get your customers to share your video content is to incentivize sharing. For example, encourage people to share your videos; remember that sharing is important when they promise to do something when the video reaches a certain number of parts.

As video content becomes so popular, it's important to remember that your brand is in danger of mingling with the masses. Creating content similar to all others' content probably gives the impression that it is different and distinctive. Developing something new, innovative, rare, and unique can help you to generate more interest in your business and thus extend the time you spend doing so.

Even if it is not always possible to create something truly unique, it can go a long way to making your video stand out from the crowd when it comes to sharing.

Market research should be a huge priority to ensure you know what you need and create video content that appeals to and relates to your audience. By connecting your viewers to your video in this way beyond mere viewing, you can encourage them to share it with their own friends and followers so they can have the same experience. One of the best ways to get more shares when it comes to social media and other forms of video sharing, in general, is to get in touch with your customers.

Why is Live Video So Popular?

While there has been much talk over the years about the importance of video as a marketing tool, this time, it's live video. Live video marketing is a form of content marketing that focuses on how your content can support your business's goals. The entertainment industry is one of the best examples of live video use to pursue business goals. Think Super Bowl halftime. So, here are some tips for developing your own live video strategy for your social media marketing.

You can use live video content to preview upcoming products, create demonstrations, how-to videos, broadcast events, and reinforce your message. Think of it as a great way to be everywhere at once!

Live video is also a great way to support your content. However, it's still important to use a website relevant to your brand's audience to get the most traffic. Ensure you see live videos as part of your marketing strategy, not just as an alternative to traditional advertising. You should also make sure you fully benefit from live video marketing benefits, both in terms of audience retention opportunities and what it offers.

Make sure people know what you're doing with live videos, whether it's advertising via email or paid advertising on social media, depending on how your budget allows it. Even if events are not part of your strategy at the moment, you can still use them to inform and connect with your customers in a new and innovative way. Users have no reason to tune in if they don't know what's going on.

One practical way to develop a live video marketing strategy is to hold monthly webinars or masterclasses, depending on the industry. Just think, there is plenty of popular media of this type out there – how-to-make videos are extremely popular in every category, from bread making to spinning pottery and creating websites.

Suppose you're trying to increase record sales or attendance at an event. In that case, live video is worth considering, whether it's a live event or an educational event. Going digital opens up the attendance options for those who can't make it in person – or in the case of quarantine, as we face during the writing of this book, enables the event to happen when it would be impossible otherwise!

Usc live video to use press releases and other written content to let your audience know that something big is going on in your business. Broadcasting a product launch or major announcement live is a fantastic way to make it available to a wider audience. You can spread what you do at a live video event by sharing it on different social media platforms; most platforms nowadays support live video streaming – in fact, the list of those that do not would be shorter!

Choose the social platforms that your business is most likely to use for any other content - this means that customers who are engaging with you on social media can take advantage of the live video stream.

Suppose live-streaming is not part of your brand content marketing strategy. In that case, you would miss out on one of the most powerful ways to reach and interact with your audience.

Let's Check Out Your Setup

The basis of a good video starts with a script, and it takes time, but if you do this part right, you can start at the production section of this list. If not, start here.

Before you start creating your video, it is helpful to brainstorm and create a written storyboard for your script to see how it works best.

You want to attract your audience's attention, tell your business in a simple, easily understandable way, and engage your visitors. That means an excellent script. Spend as much time as needed on this step!

How Are You Going to Film?

Since your video is not supposed to be live, there are several ways to record it. If you have your own camera, you can take your own pictures. Sites like Getty have thousands of royalty-free images. Or use screenshots of your own to give you instructions while recording the video and as a source of inspiration for your visuals.

Need Voiceover?

Once your script is finished, you need to take over the voiceover function, and you need an echo-free room. If you don't have a good voice, get a few friends or relatives to help you out, but you can also hire a professional to take care of the voices and the output.

If there is one thing you should buy, it is a high quality microphone. There are several good quality microphones at reasonable prices out there.

The Editing Step

Now that you have put everything together, you have to bring your project to life from here, and that is pretty easy.

Most professionals use Adobe After Effects, but there are other less expensive options like Camtasia and Sony Vegas. Both programs are relatively easy to learn.

There are many free video editing programs, but many of them are only available to businesses with a budget. Mac computers contain built-in video editing software. New versions of Windows contain a simpler but still effective video editing program.

Next, you want to add special sound effects and music, but remember that it is not legal to simply select a song and use it. There are many music websites on the Internet in which you can buy free tracks for under $50. You will also have to make sure that the music selected doesn't drown out the voices on the tape.

Publish It!

YouTube is the most popular site for publications. It is one of the best places to publish videos as soon as you are ready to publish them, and very easily at that!

Make sure your video has a good title and description, and also make sure you do the best job with the tags so that the right people can find you. The MPEG-4 format is ideal for high definition. Combined with YouTube, voila! You have your first online marketing video for under $100.

Remember, Audio, Audio, Audio!
High quality audio is one of the most overlooked pieces of content. Making a great marketing video doesn't have to cost much, and you definitely want to invest in some decent audio equipment. This alone can make, or break a high quality video.

If your camera has sound installed, make sure there are no more than three meters between you and the microphone so that everything you say can be heard. If your viewers don't understand your tone, they may not be so forgiving. Always test and adjust to find the optimal settings and repeatedly test until you find those optimal setting.

Why Influencer Campaigns are So Successful

Influencer marketing, in short, is the idea that the people who follow influencers in your niche are the same people you want to appeal to and will ideally purchase your products or subscribe to your service.

Everywhere you look on social media, new influencers appear to be emerging and making brand deals. As the number of social media influencers grows, it's hard to influence and market value when you're up against such sturdy competition.

Influencer marketing campaigns for brands become more effective when followers essentially engage with the brand, rather than the follower making a purchase without being primed beforehand; we already know this. Regardless of which engagement model you use, brands see a significant increase in the number of followers contacting social media influencers to reinforce their message and make purchases. A social media influencer's impact is measurable, which means that it helps raise awareness of your brand's products, ideas, and services.

One of the most important aspects of a successful influencer marketing campaign is defining your campaign objectives and determining your overall strategy. This is the first step in achieving your goals, and it is a key factor in the success of your influencer marketing strategy and your success rate.

By cultivating dedicated influencer ambassadors who support your existing marketing campaigns and bring influencers to market, you can successfully position your brand. By identifying the type of influence that best suits your business and developing an influential marketing strategy, your reach will dramatically improve. Putting your influencer marketing campaign at the heart of your marketing strategies is key to guiding your target audience and potential leads through your sales pipeline. Think of the influencer as a smiling tour guide leading potential customers through the purchase process.

Before you start an influencer marketing campaign, you first need to find the right influencers. Once you have found the influencer you want to work with, it is time to set it up. Suppose you remember how far the reach, relevance, and resonance of the influencer are. In that case, it ensures that your marketing campaign reaches your target audience of potential subscribers. For example, you wouldn't want to go to a toy unboxing channel to market power tools to the industrial welding sector.

Brands of all sizes should seize the opportunity to build relationships with influencers and launch creative and effective influencer marketing campaigns. Although I would never suggest copying someone else's influencer marketing campaign completely, you can learn a lot by looking at what works for other organizations, especially for first-timers.

If you have difficulty stomaching your marketing costs for social media influencers, consider that a well-managed campaign can bring you a very positive return. A recent online report shows that social media influencer marketing doesn't have to cost much. A higher budget for social media campaigns can help you take advantage of social media better than your competitors. Hire a social media influencer and watch the returns jump into the business marketing category like a wild dream.

Let's start at the very beginning; what is an influencer?

A Social Media influencer is someone with the power to influence someone's purchase decisions because of their knowledge, authority, position, or relationship with their following. They often have a following on social media channels in a specific niche.

-Nano

Nano influencers have less than 1,000 followers. They are usually local leaders, such as city mayors, heads of your local PTA, the marketing twitter of your local supermarket, ETC. – people within a set community will find their shared information valuable.

-Micro

This influencer has 1,000 to 100,000 followers. While this seems tiny, know that their opinions are strong and usually niche, meaning that people are quick to listen, as their knowledge is authoritative. If you look at the social media profiles of "talking heads" you see on the news on intellectual or scientific topics, they'll fall in this category.

-Macro

Macro influencers are the first level in which you begin to spot traditional internet celebrities. These accounts have 100,000 to 1,000,000 followers and see higher engagement levels, meaning you're likely to see these accounts sharing brand deals and sponsorships.

-Mega

These social media stars are traditional celebrities. Their account has more than 1,000,000 followers. They generally do not have a niche and are liked by a broad spectrum of individuals. Think of your favorite musical performer, then visit their social media profiles. They'll likely fit the profile.

Metrics

Whether it's influencers, marketing contracts, or the influential marketing platform you need, planning a strategy that's right for your brand can be overwhelming. The fact is that to develop an effective influencer marketing strategy for you and your business, you first need to understand how your influencer campaign works and what it means to set clear goals and metrics.

Return on Investment

Once your goals are set, your attention shifts to how you measure the ROI of your influencer marketing campaign. You need to think about influencers' impact on your business, the expected ROI for your campaign, and how it is measured.

Select Your Running Platform

Once you have chosen a platform, identify how the platform will help you collect data and what data it collects to optimize future influencer marketing campaigns.

Authenticity is Still Important in This Fake World

Like it or not, authenticity in marketing is a trend that won't disappear anytime soon. You might think marketing is inherently inauthentic, but we are in a digital age where people are so open to new ideas that our prejudices must change.

Authenticity has become indispensable. While marketing and advertising have traditionally been geared toward selling dreams, it is also about appearing as sincere and authentic as possible.

Although brand honesty may not be a new concept, the need to use more authenticity in marketing is obvious wherever you look. Authenticity is an essential part of branding, but what is the key to authentic content marketing? How do you say that, and what are the best ways to communicate authenticity, both in good and bad ways?

The main purpose of authenticity is to win consumers' trust, and this quality has considerable cultural and emotional capital. Authenticity is earned over time and is something that no imaginative marketing campaign can buy or win over a brand. Creating a genuine, lasting connection with loyal customers means presenting an authentic brand consistently and honestly. The ability to be something or someone is one of the most important characteristics of a successful brand. This characteristic holds significant cultural and emotional capital but is also a key component of an effective brand.

If you do it right, a focus on brand authenticity and connection will lead to more conversations about your brand. Conveying authenticity through content will complement your other marketing efforts, show your key audience exactly who you are as a brand, differentiate your brands from others, and put them above others. After all, developing an authentic brand strategy to show customers your honest side does not mean that you should not pay attention to the good things people have to say about you. If you want to find the right influencers to promote the brand authentically or have other questions or concerns, please contact us.

Authenticity is important for successful marketing, but it is design-driven; expressing your brand's mission through the way you do business, including advertising, ensures that marketing with authenticity is an important part of your design. Another way to produce authentic advertising is to have a strong brand identity, as you describe it in your blog, social media posts, and other media. Using user-generated content allows your marketing campaigns to work for you and your key group as a whole.

If you want to make your brand more authentic, ask what characteristics it represents and then start with authenticity's core values.

In marketing, qualitative authenticity is about answering questions about your brand and then translating these questions into your marketing efforts. Using authentic marketing is one of the easiest ways to use visual branding to create an authentic marketing experience. Content such as customer photos is called user-generated content. Its use allows a brand to stand out from a target group attuned to the brand and its message. Suppose you choose an influencer-oriented content marketing strategy. In that case, this is a great way to maximize the perception that your product is authentic to your influencers.

Another way to create authenticity in advertising is to understand the emotional attraction that your advertising message can have on your target audiences, customers, and viewers.

Neurotic and conscientious people generate more negative emotions when they see an image of extroverts, open-minded or sympathetic people in their ads. On the other hand, indexically authentic or iconographically authentic advertisements evoke more positive emotions by showing extroverts and sympathetic type of people.

If you are not trying to deliver an authentic brand strategy, you may be called upon to take a less-than-real approach. It is tempting to prioritize its content, but the apparent attempts to promote itself weaken the content's perceived authenticity. Customers love and want to connect with your brand, and if they love the brand, it's easy to get authentic content that can be used on your website or shared on social media. If you can be "authentic in everything you do and say," your customers will do your marketing for you and bypass any obstacles.

Like Cartoons?

One of the main reasons for making an animated video is that it has a greater psychological impact, according to a study by the University of California, San Diego.

By strategically animating your video marketing plan by design, your brand can better understand the masses and gain a larger customer base. Animated videos are one of the most effective ways marketers can build brand awareness and increase sales. They are all about creativity.

Animated videos are among the most effective methods available to marketers to attract new customers, create brand awareness and increase sales. Videos are a great way to capture and keep customers' attention, as animations effectively simplify complicated concepts.

An animated marketing video or explanatory video can really help reduce complex principles to simple and straightforward concepts that everyone can understand, such as the basics of a product. It isn't exactly a bad idea to get a necessary idea drilled into a viewer's head.

Whether it's a video used in a vlog or for blogging, a whiteboard animated video can cost very little compared to the enormous impact it has on your audience. Animated marketing messages are memorable because they are fun enough to share. There is no shortage of features in the hectic Internet age we live in. That shareability is a true asset.

Suppose you are looking for an easy, effective, and fast way to communicate with your target audience. In that case, there is no better way than animated marketing videos. Suppose you want to add animated videos to your marketing strategy. In that case, you can produce an animated video in-house or outsource agencies on the local, national, or international levels. Animation isn't all laminated sheets and cell-shading anymore!

The crazy secret is that live-action, at times, can be more expensive than animation.

These costs are a major reason why some companies do not use live-action videos, making animation a great alternative. Animated marketing has no limitations, so you can use animated videos to explain really complex topics interestingly. Animation is versatile and can be integrated into any marketing strategy, whether to add it to your website or as part of a video marketing campaign.

Research has shown that custom marketing videos can increase your brand's sales by an average of 20% and custom videos by up to 50%. Who can argue with the value of a 50% boost?

Are Animated Campaigns Expensive?
When it comes to launching a tempting media campaign, animated videos have proven to be pay-as-you-go, personal-animated video, especially when combined with other tempting media such as social media, video games, etc., paid-for, personal, interactive, or animated movies. Create a campaign concept optimized for a specific target group (e.g., social, mobile, online, etc.). The right audience can be drawn in like a moth to a flame.

Let's compare the resources required for each stage of production (live-action) to help you build a more informed plan for your project. Other cost factors need to be taken into account, but these are just a few of them, and you should be sure to consider them all.

Animated videos are just as expensive, in terms of cost per click. The platforms that host such ads don't care about the difference.

If you have a set budget for live-action, you can achieve even better results by allocating the same resources to an animated video; think of "buy one get one free" in the grocery store. If you use music, there is an additional cost, whether it is animation or live-action. Still, as mentioned, there are ways to negate this issue.

Remember, despite preconceived notions, animation is not as expensive as live-action – it can be an excellent alternative with a bigger bang for the buck.

Whiteboard Videos?

A Whiteboard animation video, simply put, is a whiteboard animated video. The author physically draws an illustration with whiteboards or a similar surface. This type of video is usually accompanied by a form of narrative. The script's purpose in a whiteboard animated video is to sound like it is speaking directly to the viewer.

I decided to include this list because it is not rocket science to figure out how to create a whiteboard animated video in most software. Still, there is much more you can do. "If you want to quickly make whiteboards animated movies, choose a free whiteboarding video maker and do it quickly. Otherwise, I can go to a "whiteboard animation studio" that you know can make individual whiteboard videos." That's probably what you're expecting me to say, but it is a little different.

What makes a whiteboard animated video charming to its viewers, and what makes it a compelling video style?

Part of the compelling nature is the fact that they can be complicated, featuring bouncing animations and drawings alongside music and narration, to simple – words and images drawn in real time as some music plays. They're reminiscent of our school days, that is true, but, whiteboard videos "gamify" text and images, engaging the brain differently than a flat wall of text.

If you want to use whiteboard animated videos in your campaign, VideoMakerFX is a perfect option, among others. This whiteboard animation software tool lets you create tutorials, promotional videos, animations and upload them directly to YouTube and a variety of other hosting sites.

As video content continues to take over your social feeds, you will better understand how to refine your strategy and differentiate your videos from the crowd, or well, brand-die trying. You will use the growing support of social media to share your video content. Still, you must be honest and focus on creating content that your audience will find useful. Create engaging, informative, relevant video and audio content while making it authentic.

If you can create engaging video content that makes your audience feel good, learn something, or be engaged into the "buying brain," they will come back and share it with their friends. This has its own value, as long as you create video content that truly excites your viewers.

Better still, you don't need a professional video studio to produce video content that interest your audience. That doesn't mean you have to go beyond the budget to produce the best video content out there because a little bit goes a long way.

It's crucial to see how video content is delivered and what kind of content gets maximum customer loyalty. Besides, marketers need to understand how social channels optimize their platforms to enable more video content in users feeds, and how brands use them to engage their followers. Incorporating video into your content marketing is important. Still, it is even more important to use it in the best and appropriate way. Video can take your content marketing efforts to the next level by being a powerful and effective way to spread your marketing message.

User-generated video content is a great way to showcase your brand's profound impact on the world. Video is one of the most entertaining and effective types of content you can add to your marketing campaign.

If you create engaging content, there is a good chance that you will be able to share it on social media channels. Remember that different video content types are not of much use to you if you are not addressing your content marketing in the right place. If you want to deliver results from your video content marketing, you need to take a calculated approach.

Explainer Videos

You can hire an experienced animation and video company in India to make your video, get the software, and make a stunning explanatory video, usually pretty quickly, but is it worth it?

Essentially, an explanatory video is a video that explains your company's product or service in clear, concise language. It is an excellent way to explain something in a colorful, fun and engaging way, when the subject might not be so colorful, fun, or engaging. Essentially, explanatory videos are a great way to simplify complex topics such as a company's product, service or brand line.

An explanatory video usually shows a speaker taking the viewer on a visual journey while the content explains the product or business idea. Explanatory videos capture the attention of viewers by explaining your company's products or services. As a side note, animated explanatory videos are the most popular form of explanatory videos because they are fun; they are meant to make viewers watch the entire video and therefore digest all the information.

Why Does It All Work So Well?

There are many theories about why we like live video games, but we all agree on one thing; they stimulate the brain. It's the same rigmarole for social media, movies, and even photo sharing sites such as Instagram – it's always changing, and there's always something to see.

Live content seems to have a strong psychological motivator. Our brains are generally attracted to video because it retains visual content better than words. Studies have shown that the brain stores more information when watching videos than when reading text. Optical illusions are when the visual situation deviates from the norm our brain knows, but the text does not.

The brain creates a story in the same way that it creates stories in other parts of the body, such as our eyes, ears, and brain cells. It makes a good case for video game addiction, doesn't it?

Indeed, there are several theoretical approaches to brain function, including the theory that the human brain can do some of the most mysterious things, such as generating consciousness. In fact, the idea of mentalizing the brain, known as social interaction, stems from studies in adults. Studies have shown that our brains react differently when we engage with a supposedly real person than when we think about a story or a character. Therefore, it is not clear how the brain works when you mentalize the people you interact with or what they do when there is no social interaction.

Suppose Facebook and other major brands are right. In that case, live video could soon become a cornerstone for interacting with one brand with another on both the user and corporate levels.

Perhaps the latest brain research findings can help us better understand how our wiring supports interactive videos on the web and how best to mitigate the obvious drawbacks. In a recent study published in the journal Human Brain Mapping, researchers investigated this question by examining what the brain does when people are in awe. The brain activity measured in this study is the activity that makes us see moving images. When science tells us that our brains make these stories a reality, we should be curious and seek answers - but how could that reality be wrong?

This only shows how one person's brain can send signals and stimuli to another person. Still, almost all of these signals pass from the brain to the body and vice versa.

In 2012, computer scientist Dharmendra Modha used a powerful supercomputer to simulate the human brain's development from its early stages to its state as a developed adult. The simulation was designed to simulate the brain's ability to use human brains in real-world situations, such as social interaction. This is similar to neuromorphic chips, which aim to replicate how our brains seem to grow in size as we scale from 300 neurons in a worm brain to about 85 billion in the human brain. While it may seem unproductive for the brain to cut back on what it has learned, it is possible to retrieve its high metabolic requirements by using time cells, and that is where it works.

Given imagery's immense power to change consciousness, it is natural to wonder what its long-term impact might be on the brain, but not all neuroscientists are pessimistic. Using fMRI neuroimaging, which allows researchers to map brain activity, teams could ask; "If we similarly perceive animations, what makes this happen?"

There is an extraordinary amplification that occurs whenever we pay attention to an object and become aware of it.

When light hits our retina (the back of our eyeballs), it is transformed into a signal that travels through the visual processing system in our posterior brain, which travels to construct what we see. When we look at the words and images on the page, two areas in the back of the brain are at work.

Set Goals

The important thing, to begin with, is what your goals are. What do you want to achieve from your business, and how can you use your marketing strategy to do so? This will be what you are striving to meet with your strategy. There are more examples of specific and smart goals later on, but these could give you a hint about some things that you should be thinking about achieving.

Possible overall goals to set for your social media profiles include:

-Increase brand awareness.

-Grow revenue.

-Get new traffic to your website/or other platforms.

-Increase the clickthrough rate.

-Increase mentions.

-Build a community with your audience.

But how will you achieve such things? Although they are overall goals, they are not specific, nor do they provide any real incentive. They may give you an indication, but they do not give any real inspiration for what you explicitly are aiming for. Instead, your goals should have specific numbers and timelines. Below are some ideas for sub-goals you can create; they are listed without timelines, but you should endeavor to create them.

Possible sub-goals include:

-Increasing your overall follower count.

-Increasing reach.

-Reaching x people per month.

-Increasing comments.

-Increasing mentions.

-Increasing overall likes.

-Improving your follower-to-like ratio.

-Driving traffic to your website.

-How many people click the links to your website?

-Where do these people come from?

-How long do they stay on your website?

-Growing revenue.

-Revenue from social media.

-Revenue from ads.

-Revenue from people buying your products or service.

-Growing leads.

-People using your hashtags or contests.

Goals will obviously differ for everyone, and each business will have different goals. Try to make them as specific and time-sensitive as possible; this will ensure that you are on track to meet them.

Research

The research phase of your business strategy will be incredibly important. It will be the foundation of your business, in conjunction with your marketing, which is why you need to spend adequate time getting to the bottom of your goals and how you are going to achieve them.

First, you need to research your industry. While it is likely that you have already done this—you can never be too prepared. It would be valuable to check marketing trends within your industry. This includes things like popular kinds of campaigns, hashtags, and locations to post.

You will also need to research your audience. We will discuss this more below (and throughout this Book), but you need to have a very clear understanding of who your audience is and how they use social media in order for you to be able to market to them effectively.

Additionally, you should be researching your competition. Figure out who your main competition is (both direct and indirect) and analyze their successes and their failures, and it may even be prudent and valuable to analyze their data, too. This will give you some hints of things to avoid and things that you should (and should not) be focusing on. Any advantage that you can give yourself will be invaluable; do not waste time doing things that have been proven not to work before. This does not mean that you should not take risks, but simply that you should be careful about the ones that you do take.

Audience

While it almost goes without saying, it is imperative that you understand your target audience. If you are lacking an understanding of where your target audience is spending their time online, what kind of content they enjoy, and what kind of businesses they like, your marketing strategy will not be successful.

You need to be able to paint an incredibly detailed picture of your target audience to be able to reach them effectively. You need to understand them from a demographic perspective, but your understanding will also need to include things like their income, their propensity to comment and share posts, and their geographical location. As well as understanding the times of day that they use social media. For example, there is no use posting a contest on Instagram at 10:00 am that closes a few hours later.

You also need to use the social media platforms that your audience is using. It may seem obvious, but looking into the data that shows where your audience is most online and how they use social media is the best way to enjoy a successful marketing strategy. After all, what is the point of posting if your audience does not see it? In addition to this, you also need to fill out your profiles completely, even on social media sites you may not be using. As it is better to have claimed the username and have a basic profile with consistent branding than to not. Not only does this open you to more possible searches, but it also looks professional.

The Three Keys

Your purpose, your audience, and your offer combined make up your branding. The way you present and market yourself needs to reflect all three elements to impact your consumers positively.

Once you have clearly defined all three of these, it is worth writing it all down somewhere. These make up the vision for your brand. You should check back in with these mission statements as your branding strategies progress to ensure that you are on the correct track.

You should be able to break them down into a few sentences, and it is recommended that you put them somewhere so you can refer back to it and be inspired by your branding—just as your future audience will be!

To be successful, you need to be credible. While there are a few ways to approach achieving credibility, the simplest ones are often the most effective. In this case, it is your audience, your authenticity, and realizing a level of consistency. Without these, you will not maximize the potential gains of your branding.

Your audience needs to trust you and, if your branding shows that you are authentic and consistent, they will.

Even though your audience will likely have never met you, effective personal branding makes it seem like they already know you—even though all that is happening is that they are absorbing the content you are creating.

Personal branding means that your audience will feel a bond with you; they will trust, respect, admire, and be happy to do business with you.

Retain Your Audience

The importance of appealing to your clearly defined audience cannot be overstated.

The message of your brand is not going to appeal to everyone. You need to let go of the idea that everyone must like you to be successful.

If you do not commit to a specific demographic of people, any message you create will not be as powerful. If you do not risk alienating people who are not part of your target audience, you risk not reaching those you want.

Your branding needs to be attractive to your target audience. You could have the best branding, but it will be ineffective if it does not attract your goal audience. Your brand values need to align with your audiences, and the lifestyle you are trying to portray should share similar dreams with theirs.

You need to put your brand where your audience will see it. You need to consider where they are, what they are looking for, and develop a content strategy that aligns with it.

Showcase Authenticity

Your branding needs to come across as authentic. With the rise of photoshop and influencer culture, consumers can tell when someone is showing a fake life—and they will tune out.

A "brand" does not mean a "persona." Rather, branding is a strategic showing of who you are.

Given how invasive and intertwined social media is with our lives and how easy it is to create a false impression, audiences want to follow someone real and true to who they are.

To achieve this, you should share parts of your story and be real with your audience. Sharing past experiences and future goals is a method that can be used to connect with your future consumer base—it should be done with caution; there is such a thing as oversharing!

Audiences do not naturally believe what they see or what is presented to them. They read reviews, look for multiple sources, and usually do not take things at face value. Having a strong personal brand is key in narrowing this divide. If people trust you, if you seem authentic, passionate, and natural, they will engage with your content.

In this day and age, authenticity is currency; spend it wisely.

Offer Consistency

We can discuss consistency in two ways. There is a more media-oriented level of professional consistency and then engagement consistency.

The first of these is something that can very easily be achieved. It is so simple that it instantly stands out if it is missing from your branding and makes you seem unprofessional.

It is pivotal that, aesthetically, your content is consistent. This means ensuring you have good quality photos, a recognizable logo, and a unique design that makes you stand out. You should consistently use the same colors and fonts.

Again, this can take time to set up in the beginning but will have invaluable long-term results.

While we will discuss engagement more broadly later on, it is highly advised that you have a consistent content strategy. Creating quality content takes time. You do not have to rush out as much content as possible as quickly as possible. It is better to have fewer posts of a higher caliber than many posts that are low quality and put your audience off.

Having a consistent posting schedule of high-quality, relevant content will retain your audience and inspire them to engage with your posts.

Having strong personal branding requires accountability. You need to ensure that you are accountable, not only to your audience but also to yourself. Do not sabotage your brand by neglecting to maintain and monitor your strategies.

To put it simply, the way to be seen as credible is to be credible.

Tips, Reminders, and Tricks!

Suppose you are new to the use of online marketing videos. In that case, you will be thrilled to discover how useful this technique is for building your email list and boosting sales. What beginners don't know is that you actually need to overload your videos to maximize their effectiveness. Let's see how you can give your marketing video a real boost and create campaigns.

-If you want a wide reach and presence, you need to create rich content you publish regularly. Suppose you go beyond the standard videos that everyone creates and shows. In that case, you have to go all the way back to the old-fashioned way of marketing video. For example, suppose you wanted to announce yourself with a video. In that case, we need to create a series of videos with rich, regularly published content.

-It is especially important to have a call-to-action at the end of your marketing videos, so always make sure you have it. Whenever there is an opportunity to call on your viewers to act, use them; ask them to subscribe to your newsletter, ask them to visit your blog, ask them to comment on your video, ask them to fill out a survey, or ask them to go to your website. Always ask what you want from your viewer, whether it has to do with the video itself, your brand identity, the content of the website, or even your content itself.

-The sale of your product or service is fine as long as it is relevant to the video's purpose and not just for marketing purposes. Viewers can smell a rat; it should discuss and solve the problem, not just play out for marketing purposes.

-Make the video memorable - make it different, highlight it, and create more content that viewers can relate to.

-One of the best ways to make the most of your marketing videos is to involve other people. Pay close attention to your keywords and use free tools to help you use them. You can also consider using less common but more popular keywords such as "social media," "digital marketing," and so on.

-Video is powerful, but it is much more interesting and effective when it is in the right people's hands. Get it to your target audience.

-When you sell a product designed for customers to resell and make money, let them make a statement about the money they make from your program. For example, you could ask your customers what they like about your product and what they don't like, and how they use it.

-Share your thoughts in a conversation format; share your experiences with someone else and make it some-what comedic and more interesting for your audience.

-Expand your audience by engaging other industry experts in addition to yourself. This allows you to create content based on another person's expertise, and it is an excellent way to increase the reach of your video. Trade fairs take place in almost all areas, and if you are patient, you should be able to find one in your neighborhood. If you don't have a trade fair, look around your area, find a competent local shop, or contact your local trade association.

-Make the most of your marketing videos by posting them to as many places as possible. The more pages your video is placed on, the greater your chance of expanding your audience base, and your video links will bring in more traffic. If you want to attract attention, you don't want to drag things along and waste your time because you lose focus and visitors. Contact an expert for more information on the best video marketing strategies for your business and website.

-However, the difference between a good and a superior video is only two things: opening and closing. Start with a welcome, give your company's name and capture the attention of your audience with an entrance scene that is planned as if you were making a film. The most successful marketing videos will feel like a spontaneous conversation.

-How you finish your video is very important, but make sure it is fun, surprise your audience and surprise yourself. Do something unexpected with your opening, closing, and even the end of the video.

02: Video Content Marketing

"Where a picture paints a thousand words, a video can produce millions."

-80% of all online consumed traffic is video.

-Half of today's video viewers prefer watching brand videos.

-85% completion rate compared to 58% rate with regular video.

Is there any question left to the attractive qualities of video content marketing?

360-Degree Video Experiences

To explain it simply, 360 Video is a VR-like format that allows you to view the world around you in 360-degree shots. When a viewer watches 360 videos, they can move left and right in a closed, spherical space. This allows the user to pan and zoom in on the 360-degree video to explore the full 360-degree view. The user controls his position in the room by moving his device and the distance between the viewer and the camera.

While traditional fixed-frame videos restrict the view of the location where the camera is directed, 360-degree video offers the opportunity to put you completely surrounded by seeing and hearing at the center of the action. It is more common to see footage from the real world, but the digital environment is also reflected in 360 videos. The selection of what is seen is made in real-time, as opposed to 360-degree videos. The 360 Player gives you a better movie experience and allows you to watch your favorite 360-degree videos.

There are tons of 360-degree videos on the Internet, and VR videos themselves have been very popular for several years. While VR headsets offer some of the most exciting jaw-dropping experiences, you can enjoy 360-degree videos without having VR devices, which only heighten the experience; they are in no way necessary. YouTube is also encouraging its users to use an affordable cardboard VR headpiece to watch 360-degree videos such as the Oculus Rift or the HTC Vive.

If you want to keep your 360-degree video spherical and navigable, you can also view it in 360-degree view on your computer. A 360-degree video player allows you to click and drag the video, explore it and see what it has to offer. This feature is already compatible with most video streaming platforms, especially YouTube.

Shooting a 360 Video

When you shoot a video translated into a virtual reality system, you must use a 360-degree camera. To create 360-degree videos, a camera with lenses that cover all camera angles is required, as well as a high-resolution camera lens. As you're imagining, even with modern technology, this can still be a little pricey.

The video recorded is stitched together using special software dedicated to the alignment of the various movements recorded with each camera, resulting in a 360-degree video.

Alternatively, monoscopic 360-degree videos are filmed with the field of view of a camera as a single point of view. The video is later merged into a similar-sized video. The video you record is then saved with a special camera lens and special video editing software. Producing these videos falls into a category that is a little cheaper on the production side.

At the end of the day, though, if you have the freedom to look where you want, then the action can continue in a 360-degree video.

-Suppose you really want to provide your viewers with a truly immersive learning experience. In that case, you can turn 360-degree videos into interactive, personalized mini-video games by adding 3D animations and other content to the video using a game engine or software.

-Instead of reverting to traditional video-based learning methods such as video lectures, we can use 360-degree videos (also known as immersive spherical video) to provide our learners with an immersive learning experience.

Using 360-degree cameras and GoPro rigs, you can start creating an experience rather than just a video; those are just two ideas out of many.

SEO Video?

When it comes to recording SEO videos on YouTube, it's clear that high-quality content that is engaging and informative is key. YouTube SEO does not mean adopting Google Search SEO's best practices and applying them to YouTube content.

SEO makes sure that your website's video content can be found in search engines by figuring out how search engine algorithms understand your data.

Google uses about 200 parameters to index and search, so you must focus on the goal of creating a video platform before you move on. As part of a well-rounded approach, video SEO marketing will certainly improve your video sequences.

You may not know that videos help you reach a rank for SEO, but simply put, video SEO helps you optimize your videos so that they can be indexed into the video scheme and ranked by search engines. SEO performs better because the more traffic your site gets from search engines, the higher it ranks in results and the better your video results.

Now, let's delve deeper into it and consider some steps you can take to get the most out of your WordPress videos and some tips that really apply to video SEO by improving your site, which in turn makes Google realize that you are delivering great content.

To optimize your video SEO, you should insert keywords as part of your metadata. There are plenty of online generators that can help with this. SEO best practices that should be used to find your videos are the same as the process used to optimize text content. However, we will use a slightly different approach.

Suppose your website or video is not optimized for SEO. In that case, search engines will not bother to search your pages, or video.

If you rely solely on Video SEO to rank your videos, you won't see the results you want. No matter how much you work on improving the SEO of your video, it will never get as high a rating or many views if no one is looking. The real question is if people find your content, is the video worth watching?

Before you start with video SEO, remember that it is not quite the same as SEO for written content. It can increase backlinks and engagement with your content on your site, so why not immerse yourself in it?

Edutainment!

You can integrate educational video content into branded videos that help you communicate important messages and build your business.

A teaching video is a video that shows a process, clarifies an idea, or tells someone how to achieve something best. Instructional videos demonstrate or explain a concept or show someone how to do something, such as a company presentation or a conference presentation. You've seen them both and can probably think how one of the two could help your business.

Teaching videos are not only an incredible teaching tool but can also be used as an excellent alternative for people who learn differently. By creating an educational video, you can improve your students' learning experience by giving them access to a variety of educational videos, from the most basic to the most advanced, giving students the ability to take in information at their own discretion, as well as the ability to repeat sections as necessary.

Use educational videos as part of a comprehensive public relations or educational program. It will be easier to communicate your ideas to your audience and ensure that they receive the education they want. Ultimately, creating educational videos means you can meet your customers where they are when it comes to meeting their needs.

Whether you are interested in teaching others, expanding your business, or creating online courses, educational videos are the best way to do it. You can build on this by serving consumers who prefer self-service or simply want to expand their expertise.

Drones!

Drones are great for video recording, but the simplest applications of drones can be used to enhance your marketing content, connect with your audience, and take advantage of opportunities you never thought you could. From indoor conferences to outdoor festivals, drone videos can be used for almost any event.

Why not include drone footage showing your office on your side or a funny behind-the-scenes video you took for a quick look at your day? Consider drone videos taken in the office, as they make the viewer feel one with your team and show your commitment to turning the tide for whatever problem they're looking to solve.

Of course, outside of funny videos, there are more practical elements to using drone footage.

Suppose you want to show your customers exactly what your property looks like. In that case, you should definitely shoot drone videos from the air, as drones can capture cool new angles and perspectives unavailable to us unless we suddenly grow wings. They also offer unique vantage points from which you can capture video footage uniquely and engagingly, which can greatly benefit your next video campaign. Remember, unique visuals generally earn views! Aerial drone videos also provide a great opportunity to enhance your brand at a limited cost. Great video for Facebook, Twitter, YouTube – all of those combinations!

If you want to hire a drone pilot or a drone video production company, you should make sure they are qualified for the job. If you want to take drone footage, there are costs associated with using drones, such as obtaining a license to operate drones in your local airspace. That's right, air control wants to know where drones are!

Before a drone videography company can start filming drone videos or photographs, they will need to complete the necessary formalities to obtain a commercial drone (UAS) license. They must also obtain comprehensive information from the US Department of Transportation (DOT) and the Federal Aviation Administration (FAA).

After all of this, drone videos' price is directly influenced by the quality of drone footage to be shot. For example, videos with commercial real estate drones can cost between $149 and $469, depending on how long it takes to take the video.

Thumbnail Images

This small, clickable snapshot that viewers see when they search for a video on YouTube and many other content sites, can be as important as the video text. Since a third of viewers are used to reading thumbnails on their mobile phones, make sure your own thumbnail can tell them what your video is about, even without a title.

Thumbnails will not only be visible on YouTube; wherever you embed your video, your thumbnail will display it. Since the thumbnail is the face of the video and reaches the viewer first, it matters whether someone is watching a video or not.

To understand the importance of thumbnails, you need to realize that your video competes not only with other videos on the same topic, but with any other video on YouTube. Your video thumbnail should be compelling, and users want to click through it more than any other video. YouTube video thumbnail is an important part of getting viewers to stop scrolling and clicking.

If you have a product or service, video thumbnails are a key element of your video optimization strategy and cannot be overlooked. Don't you want it to stand out, compared to others?

In a user-friendly way, video thumbnails are relevant to video marketing because they provide a great UX for your audience. Although this is often the first thing you see on a video page, it is also important for any video you have online. By taking this into account and helping to structure the displayed content, the thumbnail is a great addition to any website. Since the thumbnail gives the viewer a quick overview of what your video is all about, it makes it easier for them to control what they want to see.

A thumbnail image for each video uploaded online is one way to get a lot of attention that results in clicks. Although it was common on YouTube at the beginning not to spend much time with thumbnails, you will quickly realize just how important they are.

YouTube thumbnails have become more important over the years than the content of the video itself when it comes to the number of visits to your channel or site.

As the age-old saying goes "Never judge a book by its cover" has never been more true.

Narrative Storytelling – Yes, it Works

A recent report suggests that content marketers are rapidly expanding beyond traditional content, with video content use increasing. A recent survey of more than 1,000 marketers in the US found that 74% of them say they use video to reach their consumers.

Creating and building a unique story is a great way to leverage your brand's value as a marketer that creates a narrative. Although there are different ways to tell a story, marketers need to think about what makes the most successful brand narratives. The flexibility of storytelling allows brands to tell their stories, whether through visual storytelling, audio storytelling, or video storytelling.

For example, marketing storytelling allows advertisers to engage an audience and immerse them first while the product comes second. Marketing storytelling is different because it includes a narrative that supports the technique of showing your product positively. Stories are one of the most successful weapons for building brand loyalty, meaning that people are more likely to promote a product or brand through word of mouth marketing, which is the best way to popularize a business. That's why brands that use stories in their marketing can build strong relationships with their audiences.

Stories can help marketers make a cut - through the market, which distracts by its design and creates advertising that reaches people and sticks.

Great storytelling allows consumers to experience the personality, authenticity, and value of a brand, such as Blue Apron, which shows real, often humorous, family situations where their meal-kit offerings make a difference in the frame of hectic family life. Marketing storytelling helps consumers understand why they should care. It humanizes the brand and helps them understand the value of the product or service, why it matters to the consumer, and why they should care about it.

Narrative storytelling has proven helpful in establishing an emotional and personal connection to a brand for consumers. Video storytelling attracts people, holds their attention, and makes them feel invested in the action. When a video narrative is built around a customer pointing out his pain points on the face, it creates an incentive for the customer to look closely. The customer doesn't want this to happen to him or her, but it does, and the video storytelling tells them what to do. Think injury lawyer commercials.

Unlike commercial television, videos help tell a story. Still, they are usually heavily scripted and go beyond traditional marketing videos to evoke viewer emotions. Like commercial television, video helps tell stories. It is mostly the one that tells the consumer's story who connects on an emotional level rather than simply compliments that story. If your video reporting is primarily aimed at selling a new product, you'll need to change up the formula.

You may want to hire actors to tell stories related to your audience's most important pain points.

Animated videos are an exceptionally effective narrative tool, as they use simple visual cues to engage the audience in their stories in a way that real-life settings can't – when was the last time you saw a tub of popcorn swallow up a city? Exactly.

Suppose you don't use these elements in your marketing. In that case, you're contributing to the noise in the market rather than giving people a story to get into.

The bottom line is that creating video content with an emotional narrative will connect with your audience and increase the number of social media shares by using its search data to tell a heart-warming story.

It makes sense for many companies to adapt their marketing strategies to focus on storytelling to convey a brand message about the company to consumers. The linear approach to brand creation implies a linear marketing strategy with a single linear message and a one-dimensional brand narrative.

Get Crazy! – Strange Works

The GEICO commercial is a great example of how, no matter what you sell, you can connect with your audience and get your brand interested through inspiring videos that tell great stories, or make the viewer laugh – probably the second choice. Influencer marketing allows brands to reach their target audience in a way that feels much more authentic than traditional advertising. This targeted advertising is an advertising that adapts to changing tastes and habits of consumers. Online ads won't disappear anytime soon, and every marketer, regardless of platform, has the ability to manage a digital ad campaign.

It is really rare to see a really funny PPC ad, and the format of a PPC ad makes the humor even more impressive. Take a look at the punch line you want to deliver in your PPC ad and make sure the ad is not a joke, but actually a real product. Some may not find it too funny, but if you're going to deliver it, you're going to do it.

What people don't find funny is an advertising campaign that makes fun of people's personal purchases. Consumers will not notice a funny or weird marketing campaign unless masses of people on the Internet are sending the same message.

03: Modern Day Branding and Marketing

"Times have definitely changed..."

Customer Disqualification

"Are you a good fit for us?"

We all know that it is counterintuitive to be against disqualifying potential customers, especially in the startup sector, but, disqualification isn't always a bad thing.

We are talking about the qualification phase, when in reality we should be talking about a phase against disqualified potential customers. It is important to develop an attitude in your team that disqualifies potential customers – in fact, developing an ideal customer profile can lead our team in the right direction when it comes to disqualifying potential users.

Really, this concept can help to create an ideal customer profile that allows your sales team to identify lookalikes who have good prospects, saving your team time and boosting sales and revenue over the long term. By creating a framework that limits the best fit for each customer, your sales team can save a lot of time by no longer chasing after prospects who don't fit your profile. The earlier you can disqualify prospects during the sales process, the less time (and money) you will spend dragging them across the finish line, and the time saved for the team.

You're Out! (Disqualified Leads)

Disqualifying a lead from your sales drive does not mean that the person should not be part of your marketing campaign.

Referrals Are Still Important

Referral marketing and customer recommendations are nothing new in the business world. Still, they are often overlooked in favor of the ever-increasing focus on sales and marketing.

Today, it is common practice and a smart move to use discounts and coupon codes to generate leads and attract new customers. Discounts are not only a way to attract new customers, but they are also a cost-effective and measurable way to attract new customers, sell more products and reactivate customers you may have lost to competitors.

Giving new customers a discount makes it easy to track the effectiveness of your marketing campaign. Advertising performance can be measured in a variety of ways, including increased basket size, increased movement and revenue growth, and per-customer sales.

In a study, 78% of respondents said that redirecting customers is the best way to attract new customers. Some 44% said that recommendations were more important than acquiring other customers through different marketing channels.

Remember, too, that 66% of respondents believe that the customers referred are more likely to make their own recommendations. Customers who receive referrals have a 37% higher retention rate and 81% of consumers participate in a rewards program offered by the brand.

That's a lot of numbers, you probably feel like you're in math class, but, they point in one direction!

A customer recommendation program can be a huge advantage for your business and will expand your customer base and also increase customer loyalty. Recommendations tend to generate higher quality benefits compared to traditional marketing methods, and once they become customers, they are more likely to stick with your company. By creating an effective customer service program, you can create enthusiastic customers who will keep referring business to you, but it in the form of further purchases or recommending new customers over.

Considered a referral program?

Exclusive content, information, and guides can be used to convince existing customers to engage their friends through your customer recommendation program. Exclusive access to your community will trigger many recommendations. If you use it wisely in a customer recommendation program, you will see how traffic flows.

Another way to get customers to put your brand before their family and friends are to give them something specific to share on social media. Suppose customers share their experiences with your company on Facebook, Twitter, Instagram, Pinterest, LinkedIn, or other media. In that case, they are much more likely to engage with you and your customers through referral marketing, especially if they share their brand experience through social media.

Give Out Those Prizes!

A customer reference program offers current customers the opportunity to market your brand and spread the word about your product. They offer them a great opportunity to market their brand and communicate their products to their friends and family members.

Coupons Galore!

There are hundreds and one way you can use sales offers, discounts and deals to promote customer loyalty, acquisition and transformation. Vouchers, prizes and promotions can be used to encourage customers to buy a particular product or boost sales in certain periods. You can also measure how many new customers you receive by offering discounts on certain products, such as a discount code, free shipping or a free gift card.

One way to keep new customers is to offer discounts when current customers recommend friends or advertise for you on social media.

A discount or coupon is basically a code that customers can enter at the checkout and get a discount on their order, you know this, and have probably taken advantage of at some point!

Advertising strategies that promote various discounts and free shipping can increase sales, and promote customer loyalty in good times and bad. Promotions and discounts offer a unique moment on the customer's journey; in fact, they can enhance the customer's experience and increase sales.

However, customers who have only been window shopping may be more likely to complete their purchase if they offer a discount. Even if it is a limited offer, your new customer has a reason to try your product or service now rather than later. If it is used too often, though, it loses its effect and potential customers wait until they have a voucher. You know this too -again, we're all guilty in some form or degree!

To keep your customers updated, you can update your coupon offers regularly as customers are always looking for new bargains.

When, When, When?

Consider offering your customers birthday discounts or consider discount ideas to see how you can boost sales, increase loyalty and attract new customers without cutting into your bottom line, and this option also provides an avenue of properly timing out coupon usage.

Social Media Graphics Templates – Not Cheating

Canva is an online graphic design tool available on the Internet that offers a wide range of tools for creating eye-catching graphics and visuals - it is a graphic design tool that lets you create graphics, copies of your designs, and much more. It also offers non-designer options, including an easy drag-and-drop system for untrained designers and an in-built catalog of royalty-free images to use.

If you don't have a marketing agency to help you, Canva is a great solution. You don't need graphical skills, and you can create stunning designs in minutes, and it's as simple as that. Canva makes it easy to create a stunning design for any project; it can be created in less than a minute and with a few clicks using premade templates.

Choosing between image editing tools that can make the entire process quick and easy can sometimes be confusing.

If you just like to try out social media posts, blog posts, and other content types, then Canva is highly recommended. However, suppose you need to create a more complex design, such as an infographic or marketing report. In that case, it is not the design service you want to use.

Other tools like Adobe Photoshop definitely has more editing features than Canva. Still, it can be overwhelming and frustrating to use for beginners. Photoshop generally takes quite a lot of training or user experience before such skills become highly sought-after.

For bloggers and non-graphic designers who need to create beautiful graphics, both Canvas and Photoshop have the potential to be on an equal footing, and that is a huge advantage over the other tools out there.

Website Themes – Also Not Cheating

WordPress, Squarespace, and Wix. Do these names ring any bells?

If you are looking for a new website template for your business website from 2018 to now, they are still your best option.

Really, you have two.

In most cases, it depends on your business preferences, which are influenced by the type of website you are looking for, the size of your website, and the number of pages on your website. This is often based on your available budget. Still, in some cases, it also affects your business's preferences, such as the amount of space available on the website.

If you need a well-run website without major investment or cost, you should look at website templates. With a website template as a base, there's no need to have a developer build a new website from scratch.

In most marketplaces or app stores, you can buy a modifiable template in a variety of different formats, from HTML5 to CSS3 and CSS4, as well as a variety of other formats.

A website template can be used for any website. However, many commercial templates are often created for specific categories of websites.

The best website templates to help you set up and create in a handful of hours, and free website templates to help you create everything in a few minutes.

The Importance of Analytics

Perhaps the biggest part of social media marketing will be checking your analytics. First, it can seem like a huge task that you will never fully comprehend, but as you develop your skills, you will learn that it is easy and, honestly, kind of fun! Checking your analytics is, in effect, also a way to chart the growth of your business. Dedicating time to understanding and analyzing the data will soon spark joy-- especially if your strategy works effectively!

There are many kinds of analytics, and they are often the results of your goals. For example, three of the most common analytics will be reach, clicks, and engagement. You will also want to look into your conversion rate. This is the number of people who see your content in contrast to the number of people engaging with and giving you revenue.

It cannot be stressed enough that the only way to know if your social media marketing is successful is to check the analytics. Analytics can seem very complicated, but once you learn how they work, it will become second nature.

Some social media platforms have built-in analytics; however, there are other platforms and tools that you can use to have a more detailed, in-depth analysis. Do not feel compelled to immediately enlist the assistance of a complicated analytics tracker. You can start by using the inbuilt trackers to get the hang of analytics. You should first get familiar with the concept and things you will be looking for using the ones built into each social media site. There is no use getting too overwhelmed and neglecting to fully understand it. The benefits of using the built-in ones are that all the information is there for you already; you do not have to go anywhere else. The information is the same regardless of where you find it.

If you have already begun to post on your accounts, it is recommended that you see your progress so far—so, then you know where you need to go. In particular, pay attention to your successful posts as well as your levels of engagement--try and see how many ghost followers you have. Ghost followers are followers who do not like or interact with your content; you want as few of these as possible

Analytics include such a wide range of things. There are numerous questions that you can ask yourself and then discover the answers to through viewing analytics.

For example:

-Has your reach grown since last month?

-How was your reach been compared to last week?

-How many mentions do you get a month?

-How many uses of your unique hashtags occur?

-How many shares of your content?

-How does campaign content compare to other things you post?

-If you collaborate, how does that affect your interaction?

-If you share a post from another brand, does that other post get more interactions than your own content?

-What are your average likes?

-How many unique profile or page views?

-What is your click-through rate?

-What is your conversion rate?

-And how does it change over time?

-What time of day are your followers active?

These are just some examples of information that you can discover through analytics. You should change and develop them over time. Additionally, you should also try to set different goals for different platforms.

Additionally, the goals that you create should be SMART. That is; Specific, Measurable, Attainable, Relevant, and Time-Bound. Do not just write "increase engagement"; strive for "increase engagement by 3% in two months." As well as making them motivating, this makes it clear as to whether or not you are on track if you need to update a strategy.

Engagement
Engagement has popped up multiple times in our discussion of social media marketing because it is one of the most important things.

Engagement should be two ways. It should be your audience commenting and sharing your posts, replying to your polls, liking, retweeting, repining, resharing, or whatever it is that you want your audience to be doing! However, you also need to be engaging back with them. This means you should reply to comments like them, ask questions of your audience, and reply, as well as responding promptly to messages and emails.

It is also necessary for you to have a cohesive persona to reply to these with. While calling it a persona makes it sound like it is fake, it should not be. It should seem authentic and real. Your audience wants to feel like they interact with the person, not just a random online brand. Basically, just have a consistent voice that is in line with your brand.

Inbuilt tools

Many social media platforms have their own inbuilt tools to allow you to check your insights. This is a valuable way to understand analytics. They are simple, easy, and you do not have to use another tool because all the information is right there in front of you. Inbuilt analytics are easily accessible and, while simple, is a fantastic introduction to the principles.

Take insights on Instagram; for example, you will be able to see a breakdown of your followers' demographic, which includes age, gender, location, and their most active hours. Knowing their active hours is key to being able to post when they are online. You can also get specific insights into your posts. By doing so, you can see which posts are successful and how users engage with them; you can then apply these to your other posts.

Third-party analytics

There are many third-party analytics checkers. It can be a valuable idea to learn how to use one. Often, they run on a subscription basis or have a one-time fee. Still, they usually offer a free trial period first. One of the benefits of some of these tools is that they put all the analytics in one place for all of your social media sites, so you do not need to keep running individual checks. This will also make it easy to check your data over time and easily visualize your progress. Not only will such tools give you the analytics for the social media sites you use, but they can also give insight into relevant hashtags and wider industry trends.

Testing

Try new things and test them. Once you are familiar with the tools, trying new things and experimenting with how you post is a fantastic way to improve your analytics. The analytics will clarify which type of days are best to post on and what time of day, and what kind of engagement you generate.

Running data-driven campaigns is a central part of business, and the only way you know if something is going to work is to try it out. Nevertheless, using data will at very least give you an educated guess as to what might work.

Brand Cohesion – Your Landmark

A brand is the name, logo, or graphic design used by an organization. Although the logo is not the entire brand, it is what the brand represents visually, as it is generally the icon that the customer will recognize. That glowing yellow M in the sky, for example.

Make sure all the brand elements work together, from the logo and color palette that represents your personality to the content that reinforces values and messages to the audience at the center of it. Talk about your brand's mission through your logo and how you present your offers, products, and services.

Ideally, your brand strategy outlines the key elements that make the brand unique and how you can achieve your mission and goals. Start by creating a list of items, including your logo, brand name, logo color, color palette, and content. Ensure that these pieces of content remain consistent across the board. That means if you've got blue and white in your logo, you don't create a site with a red color palette!

Whatever your goals, your company should still strive to have a strong brand on social media. The development of a consistent brand voice across all media platforms gives your brand a cohesive feel and earns stronger brand loyalty. One of the biggest advantages of coherent branding is that your company is recognized everywhere, even where there is no logo at all. It allows you to show the company's personality and style wherever you are present, creating a strong brand identity.

Understanding your customers and maintaining a brand that consistently meets their expectations is key to maintaining your coherent brand. As we discussed, a unified brand benefits you as a company because your customers recognize you and trust you.

A coherent, well-designed brand gives your audience a mental image of your business and helps them remember it. Keeping your brand together helps them to develop a clear mental image of the brand. It is easier for you to remember visual things like your logo, logo design, and logo color scheme.

When you are working on refreshing your identity system or a new brand, it is crucial to describe how the various elements work to get the look you designed back then. If you want a consistent brand identity that stays with your customers and gives the right impression, look for ways to give your visual branded goods consistency.

If you have more than one person involved in branding and marketing your business, the best way to avoid conflicting branding is to have a style guide.

Aesthetics

Social media can be a very visual medium. Having bad aesthetic and visual elements is a number one sign of unprofessionalism. It can easily bring down a brand- especially with how easy it is for people to leave bad reviews, therefore, these little things need to be consistent.

You need to have cohesive aesthetics. This means having logos, colors, and fonts that all match each other and are consistent across your profiles. If you have not updated your visuals in a while, it may be a good thing to start doing so.

It is an easy way to update your marketing strategy. Any profile pictures and cover photos should also be the same. A potential consumer should open any of your social media profiles and know immediately that they belong to the same person.

This is imperative because brand recognition is one of the most important pillars of the marketing strategy, and aesthetics is one simple way to encourage this to occur. One way to think about this could be to look into your favorite brands and think about the associations that popped into mind when you see them; is it colors of type, a certain style of post, whatever it is, you need to have your own image. What you want people to think about you. Developing a brand vision board could help you with this and ensure that it all stays cohesive.

Voice and personality

A big part of the marketing strategy should be determining the personality and the persona of your brand. This then informs the tone of your interactions with your audience.

Some things you can think about to flesh this out specifically include:

-If the brand was a person, what is their personality?

-What is not the personality?

-Make a list of adjectives of the things you do want and the things you do not want to be associated with the brand

-What kind of relationship are you trying to build with your audience? For example, a friend, authority figure, teacher, expert, etc.

-What kind of associations do you want people to have with your business?

-Look at other examples of brands (perhaps ones that you like!) and brands similar to yours and see how they interact with the audience and what sort of person they are trying to be.

Your brand will be incorporated into many phases and areas of your business as a whole, not just the marketing strategy. For this reason, your brand is pivotal to your success

The Flywheel Model – Spin, Spin, Spin!
If you've never heard of the flywheel model, this brings us to the sales funnels' anti-thesis.

Anti-thesis of a sales funnel? Heresy!

Calm down!

In 2018, HubSpot revolutionized the traditional marketing model by switching the model to a top-down funnel and creating the flywheel model. That's where the concept was born. With clever content marketing and PR steps, they implemented the concept and thus generated many reactions.

The flywheel concept allows you to use the power of inbound marketing to attract and retain customers through a standardized and holistic process. Instead of a funnel's linearity, flywheels are a circular process that rotates and gives impetus to enthusiastic customers to boost their business. Just as a flywheel moves in a circle, think of it as 360.

It asks you to position your marketing, including sales, customer service, advertising, social media, and other aspects of your business, to get your customers to engage in word of mouth advertising – the most important kind!

This Flywheel model consists of three parts:

-The sales funnel

-The marketing funnel

-The advertising funnel

While traditional marketing funnels serve to sell leads, flywheel models focus on building long-term relationships with customers to foster growth and retention. While a funnel incorporates customers as a postscript to your marketing and sales strategy, the flywheel model focuses on keeping customers happy so they can make recommendations and help your business generate revenue. Introducing a flywheel-based model instead of a linear funnel flow not only helps your business grow but also increases sales and marketing efficiency. The benefits of using a flywheel model through marketing or sales funnel are that the former helps companies to be equipped with wheels to attract customers, feed them, promote recommendations, and generate momentum and drive steady change.

Suppose you are in a marketing funnel and have a flywheel framework integrated. In that case, you can focus on inbound marketing and use natural cycles to inspire your business to grow.

The inbound flywheel model is the perfect way to ensure that your marketing company builds lasting customer relationships and creates new ones. Unlike other marketing models that think about customer outcomes, the flywheel model thinks about customers and how they can help your business grow. The goodwill that the customer - the basis of your brand - makes up its weight in this model, while it is only an afterthought or low-level step in the others. So, when you think about business strategy, flywheel marketing is pretty important.

Customer-oriented marketing attempts to unify all aspects of the flywheel to attract new prospects and win customers. The goal of marketing flywheel is to build brand advocates who will then fuel your brand's growth. Marketing flywheels are the same, except that the forces you use are aimed at attracting, and enthusing your audience. Using the flywheel model, you see the success you have put into your marketing is used in commissions to promote growth.

In-House Advertising

One of the first mistakes people make when they hire a marketing company is to assume that marketing companies do everything. Whether to hire a team of in-house marketers or marketing managers from marketing agencies depends not only on the price but also on maximum efficiency.

The cost of hiring a marketing agency is actually lower than hiring similar teams in-house. If you hire a marketing agency, you pay the same amount as you would have spent if you hired one of the in-house marketing experts. In other words, the cost of hiring a marketing team instead of hiring a marketing expert from the company increases by about 20%.

Just think, a junior-level social media marketer will require around 30-35 thousand dollars per year in salary. This is the cost of a medium-scale project at most marketing outfits.

Suppose you have a limited marketing budget and need more help than your current employees can provide. In that case, a marketing agency can start and manage your campaigns for you. You have full control over how the agency spends your marketing budgets. You are more likely to play a more active role in the marketing process than when you work with an agency. Digital marketing agencies should be able to adapt to your needs and help you grow with marketing needs.

Even if you decide to hire in-house, you can help your customers develop and collaborate with a strategic digital marketing direction and help them grow without compromising on your marketing strategy.

Suppose you are willing to bring in professional marketing help. In that case, there are two approaches to building an in-house marketing team. If you know you are looking for marketing services, hire a marketing coordinator to train you to conduct marketing initiatives. Hiring a junior as an internal marketing generalist and empowering them to function as a fully audited marketing agency is another option – they'll create the platforms and routines before any new team members are brought in.

Alternatively, by hiring your marketing agency, you will gain greater, more diverse expertise at a reasonable monthly price. You don't have to worry about hiring new marketing staff, expanding your marketing department, or, worse, losing ridiculous amounts of money on full-time hiring.

While it may be tempting to try DIY marketing or have internal marketing staff, hiring a marketing agency will allow you to spend your money and time more effectively. Suppose you can't find the right SEO or simply don't have enough money to justify a new full-time job. In that case, a real digital marketing agency is a good alternative.

"Vintage will never get old, says the tacky sweater."

The generation of millennials, adults who grew up in the 80s and 90s, is riding a wave of nostalgia that has permeated pretty much everything in pop culture. They are becoming a consumer power to be reckoned with, and the fashion world is taking advantage of that.

Looking for answers to the question "What is nostalgia marketing? " Many companies expect a response that confirms that this form of advertising is only successful when it strikes while the iron is hot. Nostalgia marketing works because brands always keep pop culture in mind to strike when it's hottest. While some brands create nostalgia by using old-school marketing tactics, such as reviving drinks, commercials featuring celebrities from the 1980s and 1990s (I like the Command Strip ads with MC Hammer), others use creative thinking to introduce them to their brand's "storytelling campaigns."

To be honest, it is not just a good marketing strategy for these marketing departments to make consumers nostalgic for a time. You don't have to be a decades-old business to enjoy the power of nostalgia marketing strategies. Making it an emotional marketing strategy that appeals to a wider audience – Budweiser puppies fit that bill, but not Golden Girls references.

Listen to what people are saying, and incorporate these ideas into new marketing campaigns. When they listen to their audience's needs – that's when they succeed, using nostalgia as a "spice" rather than a recipe with a short shelf life.

For this reason, nostalgia marketing campaigns are becoming increasingly popular as brands begin to discover new ways to connect with their customers on a deeper and more emotional level. Nostalgia - marketing taps into new brands to return them to their original roots to be known to consumers. Companies of all ages and backgrounds combine the purpose of their brand with old ideas and evoke memories of the past, such as the 80s and 90s, and their associated brand messages. It is a way to make meaningful connections between past and present, emphasizing the old and the new.

Whether it's Colonel Sanders bringing KFC back, or millennial gamers enthusing with the new Nintendo console, smart brands can maximize nostalgia - marketing and achieve enormous results.

Researchers have made notes that nostalgia marketing is beginning to take hold among millennials and marketers because millennials are reaching the age at which they become nostalgic. Everything from fashion to music to the 1990s has a big pull, especially with the millennial demographic. Marketers use nostalgia marketing to their advantage and realize that they can combine their products with positive feelings that are already established. Nostalgia marketing is not only extremely popular with millennials but is also becoming increasingly popular with Gen Z.

While nostalgic marketing was mostly aimed at millennials and the wistful 80s and 90s, the early 2000s was used to bring Gen Zers to adulthood, especially now that the new decade is approaching. Older millennials will turn 40 this year, but the growing financial and cultural influence of the 1990s in the gaming industry is now being felt mainly on the collector's side, sending marketers toward the slippery slope of growing stale.

05: Interactive Content

"Engaging content at the highest level."

VR and Augmented Reality

While various smartphone apps are already adept at using augmented reality games to encourage a more active lifestyle, wearable augmented reality devices could take the concept to a new level by integrating health information to help people tailor the ideal workout to their fitness needs. The problem is that most of these trial concepts have flopped straight out of the gate.

Unlike virtual reality, where everything the user sees is generated by the computer, augmented reality keeps the focus on the real world and adds elements that are not really there to enhance the user experience. Augmented reality is an element that improves the computer-generated input into the "real" physical world. You've likely seen this in action already with "hologram" concerts and the card-based games for sale at specialty board game stores right now, which offer device-compatible cards that show animations on one side when scanned in.

Augmented reality's primary value is the immersive experience perceived as a natural part of the environment. Unlike virtual reality, which creates a virtual world, it does not add other digital details to the existing world, it adds new layers of perception. It combines reality and environment to the real environment, keeping the user at the center. Augmented reality focuses on the physical world and embeds digital elements such as images, video, audio, text, etc.

The simplest augmented reality use case is that the user takes an image of a real object. The underlying platform recognizes a marker that causes them to add a virtual object. Augmented reality applications running on portable devices with virtual reality headsets can also digitize the human presence in space, providing a computer-generated model of virtual space in which to interact and perform various actions. To display augmented reality, you need to use a special augmented reality app on the device to search for a specific marker or trigger image. Another great example of this is "AR Games" provided by the Nintendo 3DS.

Millennials are now the dominant consumer generation. This trend signals that AR and VR will be an exciting part of many consumer journeys. Millennials are also more interested in using digital technology and buying more digital products and services than any other age group in history.

Moreover, augmented reality now lives predominantly on smartphones. Smartphones are typically the AR devices used by most of us who have experienced AR so far. The really exciting thing about augmented reality is introducing new technologies such as virtual reality (VR), and AR could open the door to even more applications. AR can happen on any device with a camera. Still, improvements can be made using a smartphone, tablet, or even a computer with an AR camera. Most individuals own some form of a compatible smartphone.

As AR experiences become less cumbersome and more appealing, experience designers are experimenting. Soon, augmented reality experiences could be used to learn new things, like free apps, games, movies, and medicine.

Visually Enhanced Advertising?

In marketing, visual storytelling is one of the best ways to help your audience understand what your brand is all about. You can tell a story by sharing information in a way that is easily remembered. What's a commercial you'll never forget? That's right, you've got one – and why? Because of the visuals or story of the commercial – and the way it made you feel. That's storytelling – watching a movie, listening to our favorite music, and hearing a story from grandma can produce the same emotional reactions.

In the future, marketers who want to reach their audience effectively will need more strategic visuals in their marketing tactics, including online advertising and social media. More "bang for the marketing buck."

Suppose you can create high-quality visual content that really resonates with people and promote it regularly. In that case, your reputation and brand awareness will surely soar. This type of visual content can generate interest and help spread awareness of the brand rather than directly selling a product or service. Visualized, visually appealing content such as photos, videos, and interactive elements will certainly help you win customers and increase brand awareness. While any form of advertising will have a major impact on boosting your business, you should always use images and graphics.

In fact, you can add excitement to a boring old graphic or video presentation, use moving images to create interesting variations of your logo, present the service or feature you offer from a direct perspective, or even combine screenshots with your marketing copy or references to enhance your credibility. That's a basic first step, but in today's market, it will need more.

The right kind of visual content can make the difference between converting an ad or graphic and having a low impact. As we have become increasingly visual as a society, the importance of visual content in online advertising has increased dramatically. If someone is looking for any graphics or visuals, be it a video, a blog post, or even an article in a magazine or newspaper, they will follow the visual path – and that includes if the path leads to a "buy now!" message.

Let's recap a little.

-We often hear that a photo is worth a thousand words, and this idea can certainly sound true in content marketing. Visual content is everything that creates and distributes visual content to deliver content that your audience appreciates. We all know that content marketing is the process of creating value for your target audience in a way that is useful to them. Using compelling images and infographics can make an abstract idea easier to understand and more accessible to your audience.

-A great video shows that you are willing to do more for quality. There is no better example of this than the video of your company's recent product launch. Video may not be the easiest medium to master, but it is one of the most powerful marketing media ever. The ability to tell a story through visual content, be it a video, a photo, or even an infographic, is a powerful content marketing medium.

-We have described some of the fastest and easiest ways to integrate visuals into your marketing and how to get the most out of your visual advantages. Infographics are visually appealing, entertaining to look at, and very easily divisible, which helps the brain process content faster and is a great way for your brand's visual content marketing strategy to "come together."

Any graphic designer working in this field knows human psychology well enough to create a list of visual advertising techniques in order to create a good visual advertising campaign. Rejecting visual content marketing means discarding one of the most important aspects of any marketing strategy. That is the ability to communicate.

Videos

YouTube has integrated several new tools into its video authoring system that gives you the ability to hack your videos with a small amount of interactivity.

For example, the H5P Interactive Video Tool embeds various interactive video content based on the content type. You can enrich your video with different content types such as audio, graphics, music, and audio effects. If you already have a video clip that you want to add interactive elements to, H5P interactive videos are ideal for this purpose. Interactive video is perfect if you already had a video clip that you wanted to add interactive elements to.

Interactive video, also called IV, is a digital video intended to support user interaction. The term interactive video usually refers to the techniques used to merge linear film and video interaction.

By branching out your interactive video, you can let your audience choose a story they can best share with you.

Interactive videos are a great learning tool because they capture and make the viewer pay attention. Instead of just watching and sitting passively, the use of interactive videos in online learning ignites learners creativity and problem solving abilities.

Creating an interactive video with simple words can increase engagement and provide a superior customer experience. By turning ordinary passive videos into interactive videos, we can turn them into ordinary passive videos and increase customer loyalty.

The best way to learn is to just dive in and try it out, and I encourage you to do that. Interactive videos can take many forms, but I expect you will create something, so take the direction.

Interactive videos play like a normal video file. Still, they have clickable areas (hotspots) that perform actions when you click on them. Interactive videos offer viewers the ability to touch their mobile devices while the action is taking place. The viewer clicks on the desktop, and the interactive video moves to the phone or tablet and plays.

These features allow interactive videos to interact with the audience, rather than just being a passive viewer in front of the screen. Audience participation is a must for an interactive video, so make sure it's interactive enough for your audience. Therefore, interactive videos are a great way to collect data in a way that, when done right, can actually be fun.

Virtual Tours? Where are We Going?

One of the most exciting parts of creating a 360-degree virtual tour is being part of an interactive experience where you can include sound, add hotspots, and merge images and videos. A virtual tour follows the same path as an in-person tour and shows people sights, landmarks, and distances. It gives the viewer a 360-degree view of everything you want to show them along the route.

Suppose you want a more professional virtual tour. In that case, you can use a Matterport camera and app which allows you to capture a 3D representation of the environment with a special camera. Virtual Tour 360 can be used to enrich 360-degree images (H5P content).

The app provides the tools to turn your smartphone into a 360-degree camera, with the tool to create a tour in 15 minutes. If you need a designer for more creative work, this tool also offers services and design packages that help you link content and create virtual tours.

Now that you have your images and requirements, the next thing you need is to set up your virtual tour one picture at a time. This software combines panoramic photos into a 360-degree tour and merges the static images into virtual 3D tours. Now that we have our images, we can create our virtual tour by merging them with the next step's software. Once we have finished the virtual tour, your selected software will link the tour stored in the cloud.

Better still, you don't have to be a professional videographer – as long as you have a half-decent camera; it's possible to create your own necessary media. All you need to do is create an account, upload your content and share your virtual 360-degree tour with anyone you need.

Alternatively, you can use a tool like WP - VR to create a virtual tour on your WordPress site. To create your virtual tours for your website, you will need a 360-degree camera, VR headset, and other accessories (such as the Bushman 360 monopod kit), so you may need to buy or rent a camera that provides all the features you need for the type of virtual tours you want to create. Then still follow the similar formula of getting needed images and uploading them as such.

The process is actually quite simple and can regularly be seen in various industries, most prominently, in real estate. Such tours allow prospective buyers to tour properties without ever stepping foot on the site.

Crafting Website Descriptions That Matter

A meta description is a short paragraph of text placed in the HTML of a web page describing its contents. It is an HTML attribute that gives you a short, to-point summary of the website.

The Meta Description tag allows you to specify a summary of your page's content, one paragraph at a time. Meta - Descriptions are a meta tag that summarizes 155 - 160 characters describing a web page's contents.

The second description gives you clarity about what is on the page. It even provides helpful links to popular pages on your site. Imagine it as describing the page to someone who can't physically see it.

If you don't have the time to create a description for each page, try prioritizing your content. Create at least two separate descriptions for each of your blog posts and pages. If you have a meta description for every blog post on the blog, you must also have descriptions on your blog and the website homepage.

Your meta description must be unique on each web page, so make sure you do not use the same description on multiple pages. Google will severely knock down your site.

Web content authors must have the ability to insert paragraphs and headings with keywords for search engine optimization, ensure that their composition is clear, and reaches their target market. To write a good meta description of the title page, use accurate keyword phrases for each page and create and use the best keywords and phrases. A website content author must be familiar with SEO and be aware that what he writes is written by humans, not robots. Think about customers, not some mathematical algorithm.

Make sure you create a compelling meta-description for your website that convinces people to choose you over your competitors. Treat your meta-descriptions like advertisements on your websites and make them as relevant as possible to your target market. If you post a meta description as a social link, it will boost traffic and work just as well as if you post it as an ad.

If you have trouble writing a good meta description for your website, please leave it blank and let Google select sections of your website that contain the keywords you use for the search, sometimes it is better to let sleeping dogs lie than to shake them half-awake.

Even if you are not penalized with duplicate meta-descriptions, writing a clear description is crucial. It acts as a kind of sales pitch in SERP. If you fail to include the meta description of the page you want to rank for, Google will show a snippet of the text from your page's first paragraph.

Note: If Google finds that the meta described is irrelevant to your site's content, it will drag all the first sentences of the page content containing relevant keywords and still display them on SERPs.

If you follow the steps above, you can learn how to write web page content that will attract readers and search engines, generate revenue, and ensure that your pages do everything they can to help you grow your business.

Do Pop-Up Ads Work?

Google has started cracking down on pop-up ads, and they have had to rethink their installed pop-ups. We'll take a look at why pop ads can be so effective, why most people don't like them, how to use them to work with your website's traffic, and more – plus how to deal with Google!

As you may have noticed, the statistics speak for themselves. Pop-up ads are not only annoying but can even redirect you to malicious sites and cause serious problems for users – our visitors know this; they're already primed to not enjoy seeing them.

Even though most people despise pop-up ads, you can create valuable pop-ups that your page traffic will actually appreciate. With the right approach, we can create a pop-up ad that helps us mitigate even more conversions from our website's traffic. While people seem to respond to pop-ups and ads, you will frustrate both your site's traffic and Google if you don't use them properly. In fact, Google wants you to create more conversion on your site, and they acknowledge the role that popups could play in that.

Pop-ups need not be disruptive, invasive, or distracting. They can be used as a complementary tool in your content marketing efforts as presented. Pop-up advertising works best when it appeals to your website's visitors and improves their experience, not annoys them.

While pop-up ads work well to turn visitors into subscribers, they may hurt your SEO because of their negative impact on the user experience. It can be weighing the greater evil.

The problem with pop-up ads is not necessarily that the ads themselves are poorly embedded. Still, it is that most marketers don't know how to use them effectively. The right way to do it, is for advertisers and brands to make them work for them. Before sharing my experience with pop-ups on an e-commerce site, let's briefly determine why people actually avoid pop-ups in many cases.

According to the Blog Marketing Academy, the pop-up click-through rates are about 2% higher than any other type of advertising. Pop-ups generally have a higher click-through rate than other advertising types, such as ads on social media sites. Despite their nervousness, pop-up ads have an average click rate of about 1.5% per click. Although people seem to despise them, marketers continue to use them because their users respond to them repeatedly. Popups generally have a much lower click rate (about 0.7%) than the average ad.

According to Search Engine Land, 70% of US users are annoyed by pop-up ads. The main reason for blocking a page is an annoying ad. In terms of advertising, these statistics are revealing. Still, marketers are aware of the knee-jerk negative reaction many people have when they see one.

You can use pop-ups that don't look like they've been seen anywhere else, such as Facebook, Twitter, and other social media sites – that will help with the aggravation, making it something new rather than old-hat.

If pop-up ads are professionally designed, and you pay attention to what the call-to-action button says, they can help you get good results.

Quizzes and Polls

As popularized by BuzzFeed, online quizzes are great, but with a few exceptions, are largely made by adults for entertainment and novelty purposes rather than actually collecting information. "What Frappuccino are you?" might, and it is a small might, have some value for Starbucks, but that's about it.

Other websites use quizzes to see how long and for what length they keep readers on the site. There are many places in the US where you can find online quizzes galore, such as the New York Times, the Huffington Post, and the Washington Post – they are using quizzes to collect this information to retain readers on their site for longer periods, as it is the news business – to keep those subscriptions going, users need to be kept reading.

Suppose you can trust online surveys to tell you how people really feel. In that case, this is a fair way to go, but if you don't want to limit yourself to a BuzzFeed-style quiz, consider personality or quiz questions, even quiz questions on a particular topic.

-Do you have these symptoms? Our pill may be right for you.

-Not sleeping well at night? Try our new mattress set.

In these quizzes, users understand the importance of communicating their findings in a meaningful way, not just in the form of a question and answer session. They're using their answers to reach an ultimate goal – "will this product or service help me?"

A sample of a large group of volunteers is taken from this. The results are weighted to reflect the demographic development of the population and its interests. Common uses include gathering information on demographic factors such as age, gender, race, ethnicity, religion, education, and quiz rankings.

The Center for Media Engagement has found that online quizzes have many benefits; they encourage people to spend more time on websites, leading to more time for the visitor to take action.

Also, a standardized online quiz can help keep track of when consumers are finally ready to buy. It encourages them to learn and it's fun.

While surveys on social media are often a good way to gather additional data about your audience and liven up your presentation, you need a more robust tool for gathering feedback. There are numerous pieces of software, such as Poll Junkie, that help you create a quick and free survey by registering for an account. For example, if you are conducting a Twitter poll or straw poll that provides real-time feedback on a particular topic, such as the current business status, you will need to provide it with a link to your Twitter account, email address, phone number, in exchange for that complex book of opinions at the finish line.

Links

When it comes to content and search engine optimization (SEO), one thing has absolute priority; URLs.

I have come to the conclusion that URLs are clearly important. Still, when it comes to SEO, I consider them to be a key component that search engines index through your content in the first instance.

URLs are also the incoming links that search engines search to identify your site's most important pages. The URL appears in the search engine results and tells users that your site is of legitimate interests; they are more likely to click on this link. Creating page content that matches the URL of the page title and page titles that match the URL will give you more credibility with your audience. They will know that it matches your website's content.

URLs, if they are meaningful and reflect the content of the page they lead to, can make it easier for your users to visit your content. URLs are easy to type, which makes them informative and as easy to use as possible; this is useful to ensure repeated visits to your site. By taking the time to design your URLs and make them informative, useful, and easy to remember as you use them, you can increase page views and resources. SEO Boost, filtering by common keywords in older URLs, can also ensure that your old URLs match new ones.

While the right URL structure is not exactly the Holy Grail of SEO efforts, it can serve as a great tool to better understand your website and your users' content. Keyword integration and URLs' readability can improve your results, but they are not the only important factors.

When it comes to optimizing URLs, it is important to ensure that they follow the same rules and consider up-to-date best practices.

Ideally, the part of the URL that follows the domain name should contain the keyword alone. Some search engines, such as Google, omit these words as unnecessary, so it is best not to include them in your URL.

Let's try an example:

-Pets.com/orderdogfood

-Pets.com/aidaohfeuniae

Which link can I go to for buying dog food? In our example, you can order dog food at both, but only one is structured properly.

As a publisher, I trust short URLs rather than long URLs and tend to avoid links to long URLs. Besides, it is obvious that other webmasters and bloggers link to your site with a short URL rather than a long one, so we as publishers trust shorter URLs. A study by Backlinko suggests that there is technically a limit to 2048 characters for URLs. Still, in practice, they should be much, much shorter. Moz software suggests keeping the URL below 100 characters. TinyURL allows you to customize the last part of the URL to keep it active forever, even though it is technically not even shorter.

Even better, plugins like Pretty Links can halve the work required, make it much easier to format your URLs, and can be used to improve their impact on SEO. You can easily view your entire link history, edit or delete the desired URL, or use the administration, filtering, tagging, and search functions to find the desired URL.

You can track the connection to your links using the URL shortcut, create custom short links, and make improvements to your marketing campaigns. To create highly targeted, word-based URLs that direct traffic to the site and encourage people to convert, test the beta version of Smart Link.

Call to Action

A Call to Action (CTA) is defined as a message that invites the user to perform a particular action and is basically a way for the user to take any action that the page owner wants.

It is a message on the page that encourages the visitor to take the next step, carry out the action, or vice versa.

A good call to action should be clear and concrete, generating an urgency that drives users to act (e.g., click, read, learn, find, check).

Calls for action like this let consumers know that they are ready to respond immediately to their needs. Adding "now" to the CTA button is a great way to repeat what this means. Calls to action tell users exactly what to expect and are therefore aptly named. A call-to-action button tells users what they can get before they perform an action.

-Click here to subscribe!

-Look for the coupon!

-Sign up now!

A clear and convincing call to action can steer users in a direction that helps visitors and site owners to achieve their respective goals. An effective website with calls for action will act as a catalyst for interested parties to take additional measures beyond what they have been looking for. By giving visitors a way to achieve their goals and making things easy and convenient from the start, calls to action make websites much more efficient.

If you have visitors on your site, calls to action are the next logical step in the conversion process.

This tactic encourages your visitors to become active on the website, seeing what "rabbit holes" they can journey into.

Try More Than One

The purpose of the second call to action is to attract the attention of users who did not find the first call to action as attractive. Still, the second "call to action" sounds exactly like it is; you are literally asking your audience to take a particular action, maybe a little more desperately this time, as it could be your last chance in said session.

06: The Modern Day Website
"Websites have evolved."

Core Web Vitals?

The simple definition? Core Web Vitals refers to what Google is looking for in terms of a website's user experience. It's a factor that's part of Google's Experience Score page, which evaluates the total number of UX sites.

It does not take into account the technology or architecture involved in providing the experience. Core Web Vitals measures the user experience of a website's user interface, such as layout, layout design, and navigation. All three are the most important factors in Google's central measurement of weaving experience.

From 2021, Core Web Vitals will also take into account the speed of the website. Developers will also be able to report on it by writing code through the Web Vital library that they can use to measure and display metrics while browsing the web. Google will measure it in a variety of ways, such as defining the page experience. Even if your analytics provider has built-in support, those that do not include basic or custom metrics and features that allow you to measure them with your tools should.

Here we take a look at why core web vitality matters, the latest metrics introduced by Google, and how you can work to monitor and improve the vital signs of your own website. The following web vitalities break down several metrics that are used to measure loading power:

-Interactivity

-Visual stability

-Amount of site content

As you can imagine, all of these pieces are crucial for an excellent user experience.

Google considers your website's user experience to be the most important factor in its web life data.

What's With Load Times?

If you're not satisfied with the processing speed of your website, the next section will reveal ways to improve the loading speed. The goal is to match the loading speed recommended by Google.

This information gives you the ability to assess your website speed and provides concrete measures you can take to make improvements. The initial speed of each page is monitored by tracking the number of ping requests on your website server. The loading times can also affect your ranking on a website, as well as the number of visitors.

A fully loaded page indicates how long it takes for 100% of all resources on the page to be loaded and also gives you an idea of what the biggest elements are that will affect the speed of your website the most. This gives an estimate of the total number of pages that will be loaded in total, as well as the number of resources on each page.

The average e-commerce site can take seven seconds to load, and Google is now penalizing websites with slow loading times. A full-page load time includes all the images, fonts, CSS, and code needed to capture them, as well as the total number of pages on the site. Any website with a fast load time that meets the recommended load time will receive a higher SEO ranking.

Before you start a website speed optimization, you should specify your current load time and define what slows down your website. You should conduct a thorough technical SEO check and visit all the elements that can affect the page speed of your site.

The download time of a website, also known as page load time, depends on the amount of content and assets that are downloaded from your hosting server to your requesting browser. HTML, images, and other content needed to load a fully functional website will affect your entire page load time. For example, if you have a file that is larger than 150 bytes, the download takes longer, slowing down the loading of each page.

Page speed or load time is the time it takes to view the content of a particular page on a website. Page loading speed is determined by several factors, including page size, page layout, and page count. Simply put, the average time it took for a page to appear on your screen.

Before you start debugging to optimize the speed of your site, you need to know what you think is the best time to load your site. By optimizing critical render paths, you can ensure that your users have access to the fastest possible page load times in real-world scenarios. There are many different methods for determining the average page load times, which means that it is possible for web development teams to focus on streamlining the slow load process.

It is also a well-known fact that Google considers the loading time of websites as a ranking factor. Since Google uses page speed as a key factor in page placement, slow page loading can have a devastating effect on search engine optimization.

Blogging – What's It Good For?

A blog is one of the easiest ways to generate a regular stream of effective SEO content. That in itself makes it a great strategy for your website, but what's even better is that you need to focus specifically on the SEO aspect to make it work. If you optimize your blog posts well for SEO, your website will be listed faster on search engine results pages, and more people will be able to get to know your business and learn about the site.

A blog can be one of the most effective ways to market your website in search engines, and we know that it can also help you rank it higher in the search engine. Optimizing blog SEO will not only ensure a higher ranking in your search results but also a higher number of new visitors and new high-quality traffic that attracts new, high-quality visitors to blogs and websites.

Anything you do to make your blog more attractive to your audience will only help to increase your SEO results. In-depth blogging helps improve SEO in a variety of ways that increase search results, and in terms of SEO, it can help increase visibility in the search engine by expanding keyword searches and helping with a number of factors that can positively impact your organic rankings.

You should make sure that every other piece of content on your site also refers back to your blog entries. In addition, you might also include incoming links from your own site embedded in each blog entry to help search engines understand what your site is about. The use of links to other websites, such as your personal website, will help validate your blogs posts with search engines. You'll be all the better off if you plan to link all your blogging posts and your SEO checklist with an internal link.

Ask your blog authors to link to their social media accounts so you can improve how your posts on search engine ranking pages look. When you create a blog post, one or more indexed search engine pages are created, which means that traffic is directed to your site. If you share your new blog posts on your social media profiles, you will also create more backlinks on the website, and this will further boost your SEO. This works because of their indexing. So once the blog is indexed on the machines, it stays there, meaning it can still gain traffic and generate leads for you for weeks or months.

The benefits of blogging for SEO can also be seen in the way search engines such as Google and Bing search websites as they grow. This means that not only does it increase traffic to your website, but you also need to regularly update the content of your blog and website and create more backlinks to it. One of the most important aspects of a good blog structure is the ability to simply note content that is not to be indexed by the search engine.

Before we go into the more technical aspects of blogging for SEO, I would like to point out that search engines often change their value. So before you write an SEO-friendly blog post that pops up in search engines near and far, you need to think about how you can market your content. If you want to optimize your blog to help with SEO, you will want to check out the Google SEO Starter Guide and subscribe to Google's official blog.

Improving local SEO through blog posts means that you have to write useful topics that will appeal to your audience, not only for your blog but also for search engines. Improving local SEO through blog posts means that you have to write useful topics that will appeal to your audience, not only for your blog but also for search engines.

Incorporating YouTube Vlogging – Why?

The YouTube blog is a platform for original content creators to connect, inform and inspire worldwide. Blogs contributed by YouTube users are the second most visited site in the United States, behind Facebook. That's a whole lot of eyeballs.

Interestingly enough, quite a few people are gaming vloggers YouTube personalities who stream video of themselves playing popular video games – often with strange or funny commentary. While it is a fairly new phenomenon in comparison with the life of YouTube itself, it neatly brings us to one of the most interesting aspects of YouTube, the blogosphere.

When YouTube started, it all started with its first YouTube stars, and it was considered home to much more than just vlogs. In fact, you could say that the leading YouTube vloggers shared their lives all the way down to the bank. YouTube celebrities such as Fred, LonelyGirl, Zipster, Nalts, and others paved the way, sharing content from skits to gossip and the doldrums of daily life.

When it comes to posting videos on YouTube every day, it doesn't hurt to know the best time to post on YouTube. This will help you ensure that your audience is active and more likely to watch your content. Another way to be sure that your viewers are connected to your channel is when they log in to see what new videos you post. YouTubers are advertising new videos to their audience, so even those who don't subscribe to their channel will still know when a new video will appear.

If you're in the fashion world, for example, Instagram and YouTube are probably the most popular platforms for your audience. Sites like YouTube can become valuable resources for brands, marketers, and creators, giving you a taste of what's currently popular.

You can create videos that target emerging YouTube trends to ride the wave and attract more video subscribers. For example, you can record a video with your smartphone, upload it to YouTube and use the YouTube feed on your blog.

So the channels with the most subscribers on YouTube tend to be the game channels, and PewDiePie (46.7 million subscribers) last year saw the highest number of subscribers of any game channel. Sports channels on YouTube are aggregated content from other YouTube channels and share content with other channels.

Generally, it is quite easy to get views on YouTube, even if there is a lack of video content in many niches.

Do You Know How to Work PPC?

According to a recent study, almost 50% of small businesses already use pay-per-click advertising (PPC). Internet companies have realized a significant increase in the use of paid clicks - through advertising in their business model.

Don't confuse these for banner ads, these are ads for related content that appear in the ad but are not normally paid for by clicking – advertisers instead pay for them to live on a site for a specified amount of time. The difference with PPC advertising is that you only pay for the ads when a user clicks on them, not every time they click on an ad.

Each time someone clicks on a PPC ad, the company pays a fee, no matter how many times it is clicked, those charges accrue. If you have a pay-per-click account with Google Ads, you will see these ads in your Google search results.

If you already have an existing Google Ads or Microsoft Advertising account, your team can start paying instantly with a click. Now we delve deeper into the question of how to set up a paid - per - click marketing campaign with Google ads. If you decide to attract traffic by paying an amount for each click of a visitor, you can maximize the effectiveness of your payment.

Crafting Those Perfect Keywords

You can choose which keywords you want to offer, and this allows you to save ad fat by choosing exactly what you pay for and what you don't. One of the most popular ways to pay for clicks is perhaps to "pay" for someone actually clicking on an ad and redirecting it to their page. This is perhaps the most effective advertising strategy for any Internet-based company.

Advertising with a PPC program like Google Adwords is not an easy thing, as many gurus tell you in sales conversations. In fact, it can be extremely difficult, if not impossible, to achieve a reasonable return in certain niches of pay - per click of advertising. It is like paying for a billboard that could generate many impressions but few actions.

But if you follow a few basic principles, you are guaranteed to get an excellent ROI with PPC advertising. So where do you start, and what are some of the key elements of a great PPC display?

Writing an ad that increases your click-through value (CTR) is probably a good start, but only as good as selecting the right keywords for your ad.

If you want your ad to click high - by the rate, focus it on key phrases that use the same root keyword. If someone searches for one of these keywords, the display should appear bold, because the root is part of the keyword searched for. This allows you to repeat the "root" keyword 1-3 times during the entire display. The first and most important step is to make it look as if it has nothing to do with writing your ads.

Also remember to include keywords in the headline to make them stand out more, here you just want to offer a product or service. People need to see immediately whether your ad is relevant or not, so focus on the keywords and not the content.

The best way to communicate this is to clarify what you are selling, and who you are selling to. Here you do not explain what the product can do for the person, but you share the best related characteristics, such as the price, benefits, etc. Finally, in the second line, you communicate what benefits are associated with your products.

Your product could be as simple as saving hundreds or as complex as teaching you how to make "millions" with your new product, such as a free e-book or a special offer.

Ask yourself (and possibly a friend) what would make you take action, and if so, what action would you take.

Once you've placed and shot your first ad, you'll want to start testing competing ads. Start by changing the heading to get a better CTR, then work your way up to the first line and then to the second line. The best way to do this is to change parts of the display constantly, so start testing.

After a few weeks of working on these changes, you should have an effective and powerful display and you are ready for the next step.

Tracking Campaign Results

When it comes to business, it is vital to be able to track the impact of your decisions, testing and tracking data is crucial. However, it is vital that you understand the impact of all these decisions.

When it comes to payments and clicks, you have a unique opportunity to test and track everything. There may be no other form of advertising that can be so easily tested and tracked, but PPC testing and tracking are one of the most important components of any advertising campaign, and for this reason you should think about constantly improving them. The first level is to test - and track - the effectiveness of your advertising campaigns.

In all the above situations, conversion rates are included in the tracking component, but they are more important than any other metric. How many people have seen a particular ad you have placed, and do you know if you can compare multiple ads to see which one is the best?

Next, you want to track and test your sales page, and again the conversion rates are determined. This check comes when you slowly tweak the heading of your PPC display or test different elements to see what works best. Finally, it should depend on whether your ad can be improved substantially. All these tracking and testing are determined by the number of clicks on the display, not only by the conversion rate, but also by other metrics.

There are other metrics, such as how many sales are made per 100 visitors, how many click-through rates and so on. There is also a lot of information about the number of clicks on the display and the conversion rate.

If you already run a profitable PPC advertising campaign, you can improve your profit margins, but you need to know where there are errors or glitches in the system. You may want to reformulate your other ads so that we can clarify which traffic is unlikely to be converted. If that's the case, can you afford to spend more money on different ads? Is the number of people searching for a particular keyword and clicking on it more likely than the number of people searching for other keywords and clicking on another ad, or is it a sign that they are looking at another keyword?

Are you paying too much for certain keywords and choosing the wrong keywords, or are you on the sales page and paying for the right keywords?

In some cases, you may need to find out if you want to increase your profit margins, but certain ads will not be delivered as expected.

Fortunately, Google offers a number of tools for AdWords advertising that you can use to track and test your PPC campaign. You can monitor your campaign statistics and insert code on your sales page that allows you to track your visitors behavior so you know everything visitors do, from the time they view your ads to the times they buy, and so on.

Testing and tracking may not be easy, but it is necessary, and if you already run a profitable business, you should consider it as a way to increase your profit margins.

At the End of the Day, Organic Traffic Still Wins Out

In general, traffic from search engine optimization has proven to be quite cheap, and it takes very little time to optimize it. The traffic that should be generated by search engine optimization leads to a result that is considerable - the traffic of search engines.

If you take the time to create relevant content, use the right tags and share a few links, you can put your site at the top of the search engine results. This is only half the price, but relatively inexpensive compared to the cost of a click, which could cost several dollars per visitor.

Apart from being cheap, organic search engine traffic is good for a number of other reasons, but an obvious reason is that you do not have to spend time monitoring the flow of organic SEO traffic for fear of overshooting your budget. You can check your AdWords account and other PPC accounts to see how well your ads work.

Organic search engine traffic is different, but the less time you spend thinking about how you actually generate traffic, the more your visitors benefit. Instead of looking at statistics every day and thinking you have a win, you can add your own wages.

One of the biggest advantages of using organic search engine traffic is that it tends to convert better. In fact, many experts would argue that it is much better to convert your links into sponsored sections before they are in search engines.

As the first non-sponsored result that appears on Google for a particular keyword, this alone will give you enormous credibility. People tend to see anything as an ad rather than a sponsored link in search results.

That means that if you are at the top of Google by keyword, there is a good chance that your site will link to you because you are considered an authority in this area. In a way, a higher search engine ranking can generate itself, but it tends to generate higher rankings. This will consolidate your top position and also improve your placement in other keywords. After all, this is one of the most important aspects of high ranking in Google search results.

There are no hidden or sponsored links, but there is organic search engine traffic that can be used and it will cost comparatively less. Because it's not really free, it takes time and you have to be consistent. But there are other ways to use it that you could use for yourself.

07: Podcasts

"Podcasts are in their prime."

Podcasts are extremely popular, and according to a recent study, 30% of people listen to podcasts at least once a week. Podcast studies also show that 212 million Americans have heard of podcasts, while 155 million of them have heard them. According to the Pew Research Center, more than half of those who have never seen a podcast listen to it more often today than they did a year ago, compared to just over half a decade ago.

Studies show that Apple's podcast service is listened to by more than 1.5 million people in the US alone, up from just over 1 million a few years ago.

A survey from August 2019 found that 90% of podcast consumers in the US prefer to listen to podcasts at home. In fact, nine out of ten podcast listeners in the US say they listen to a podcast from home, and a high number of listeners (74%) agree that they have listened to podcasts to learn something new. It was also found that frequent podcast listeners are more likely to use multiple types of devices to listen to podcasts than non-frequent listeners, and in the age of stay-at-home orders, this means potential goldmines!

Creators and consumers are only one part of the equation, as podcast platforms also help to increase the availability and discoverability of podcasts by making it easier for everyone to find and listen to the podcast of their choice.

Podcasts are free to produce as well as consume, and there are podcasts that cover just about any interest. The enthusiasm of podcast listeners has led to many fanatic followers of podcasts and has even sparked online message boards and Reddit groups of fans. The familiarity of a podcast is a very important thing; even if it means that many people aren't consuming it, the existence of a podcast indicates credibility. Podcasts are just as attractive for those who simply enjoy a variety of different media such as video, audio, music, and social media.

While people find podcasts in many different ways, 72.8% of people agree that finding fresh and unique content is the biggest challenge. Many podcasts rely on paid marketing through more popular or similar podcasts, as well as the hosts being interviewed by more popular podcasters.

Podcast Beta is a searchable compendium of podcasts that allows you to browse through each one and rate it from highest to lowest. Feedburner lists more than 58,000 podcasts and also offers a podcast blog. This network provides access to the most popular podcasts, including your content, as well as a list of the top 10 most successful podcasts in the US.

The most common podcast topics include comedy, news, politics, and sports, so those interested have plenty of options.

If you are an iPhone user, it is even easier to subscribe to a podcast and listen to it weekly or even daily through iTunes. Whatever you're interested in, podcasts are one of the most popular forms of entertainment available on the Internet today. Listeners can listen online or offline and subscribe to their favorite podcasts.

08: The Social Media Pandemic

"Forget what you think you know about social media!"

Influencer marketing is not a new concept, but it still leaves many entrepreneurs confused. In five years, it could be drastically different from today, and the influencers will stay. The world of marketing, from advertising to marketing strategies, business models, marketing tactics, and more, has changed greatly in such a short time.

In many ways, advocacy marketing is the same as influencer marketing, but the real difference is that it's about existing customers and what those customers tell other people. At a fundamental level, influencer marketing is social media marketing, where people are employed who have a dedicated social following, who have had or will have experts in their niche, and who consider themselves "influencers."

The point of micro-influencer marketing is to reach a very specific audience that has a great conversion potential. Micro-influencers are able to create a strong bond with their followers. They can interact with them on a daily basis and engage with them without having to devote an episode to them, and they can engage and interact with them in a way that their engaged followers cannot.

There are no strict rules that dictate an exact number of followers, but most marketers consider a micro-influencer to be a person with 10,000 followers. You only have to look at the number of followers you need to have to see if they have less than 100,000 followers (based on TapInfluence's definition of micro-influencers).

Although the exact definitions vary, a micro-influencer can have up to 10,000 followers on a single social platform. If your views diverge, you might consider them a macro - an influencer who can have a few hundred, a thousand, or a million. For example, if you have 1,000 - 40,500 followers on all your social platforms, your micro-influencer could have between 1,000 - 50,000 followers and vice versa.

The cost-effectiveness of micro-influencers also means that brands can choose to work with several of them at the same time and reach a more engaged audience in the long run. It's a win-win solution.

As they are the rising stars of influencer marketing. As a result, micro-influences have become a key element of many brands' marketing strategies and strategies.

Celebrity Distrust

One of the reasons influencer marketing has become so popular among marketers is that they need content – more than can be provided by small in-house teams, usually strapped for budgets. User-generated content is a solution to the problems that marketers face with growing consumer distrust, which is why it has become such an important part of their marketing strategy and business model.

This has led to many brands changing their thinking from striving for the greatest possible reach to a transparent quality of engagement. Many brands and agencies turn to influencer marketing to reach their audiences with the voices they trust most.

This trend has proven more effective than traditional marketing because consumers are more likely to engage with messages from celebrities whose personalities they know and trust.

You know this – your favorite singer or movie actor, smiling, using a product. George Clooney sipping an espresso from a machine, or Michael Jackson sipping a Pepsi.

While this tactic worked in the past, this tactic has begun to wane in current times.

One way to increase trust in brands is to improve transparency, which will certainly affect influencer marketing campaigns. Many marketers forget why influencers are influencers; people trust their recommendations and are interested in the content they publish. They feel more authentic than movie stars, who are known for being "fake."

Viewers who are skeptical about advertising tend to transfer attention from celebrity endorsers to brands rather than from brand information presented in ads. As the time spent watching advertising increases, attention resources are used more on brand and brand information advertising than on celebrity advertising. The celebrity becomes just a face as effective as an extra from the background.

Not surprisingly, 39% of marketing professionals say they will increase their influencer marketing budgets this year. Studies have noted that 73% of marketers have a budget specifically for influencer marketing, and 84% plan to implement it over the next twelve months.

The big idea is that if you're not comfortable using influencer marketing to do social media content marketing, you're doing it wrong. What Instagram and YouTube influencers are proving is that for consumers, the humanity of influencing marketing is the most engaging aspect of the practice.

Better to Go with Authentic, Real Users

There has been much talk recently about authenticity in marketing, as consumers are wary of traditional marketing techniques. Like it or not, it is a trend that will not fade away any time soon. You might think marketing is inherently inauthentic, but we are in a digital age where people are able to change our prejudices in the digital age.

Over looking authenticity in your content such as cutting out expensive celebrity spokespeople will complicate your other marketing efforts. Set your brand apart, and show your key audience exactly who you are. Showing your audience why you do what you do and what makes you a brand that is authentic and relevant to their lives will help consumers feel a personal connection with the brand.

If your customers' attitudes don't align with the values you want to promote, your company's efforts at authentic marketing will be in vain, just as well if the attitude of your brand and employees is not in line with the values you promote, you will waste all your efforts on inauthentic marketing. For example, you can't imagine environment-loving customers or employees wildly supporting a corporate petroleum mega-giant.

You sacrifice authenticity when your marketing message is not in line with the values of your company, your employees, or even the values of your brand.

If you want to attract more loyal customers, authentic marketing is a key aspect of your sales strategy. If your goal is to make your social media marketing success in generating revenue and growing your following, you need to move with the times and incorporate the storytelling of your brand. That's why true marketing goes hand in hand with strategic marketing, and it's about choosing an audience that suits your company's goods and services.

Authentic content marketing allows you to show that you are in touch with your audience's interests in an unpretentious way. It shows that your brand is able to give your customers what they want and need, and it increases customer loyalty by providing real value. Consumers are actively seeking dialogue with brands, so if you want to, you can take on the challenge of authentic content marketing to grow your business's customer base and brand.

If you can be authentic in everything you do and say, your customers will do better with your marketing and get around potential obstacles. If you ask them to invest in your product or service, they will find that it is knowledge, entertainment, and positive emotional feedback; that's what they want. Unlike generic content marketing, authentic content marketing gives you the authenticity of who your consumers are and gives them a better chance to buy from you.

This may seem obvious, but if you want your customers to perceive you as authentic, you also need to be authentic. Authenticity builds consumer trust and loyalty, and you can achieve this by delivering brand equity, sharing brand equity, and consistently communicating your brand's history. If you are authentic, you need to combine authenticity with truth because customers want their experience to match the product or service they offer. Don't try to portray something that you think savvy consumers will feel; if you fake it, behave more authentically, and they will come to you to invent it.

On the other hand, campaigns using authentic marketing are much more interlinked, but remember that you are creating a semblance of kindness. Authentic marketing campaigns are not what you have worked on in the past; they are not what makes other people successful. Add a personal touch to your influencer marketing videos, and you will look more authentic than the influencers in your audience. If you are authentic in marketing, start using real images of your employees to create a lasting connection with your audience.

In marketing, qualitative authenticity is the ability to answer questions about your brand and then translate these questions into marketing efforts. Authentic marketing means finding out why you personally believe in your product and then passing that message on to your potential customers.

It reflects your personality and soul as an entrepreneur and asks:

"What does my brand believe in?"

Social Commerce – What's That?

A concept that has emerged at the interface of social media and e-commerce is already changing the way people shop. From simply adding a purchase button to a social media post to user-generated content, social commerce has become an integral part of the consumer's shopping tour. Social commerce is e-commerce that uses online media to support social interaction and user contributions to improve the online shopping experience.

Although e-commerce and social commerce can easily be confused, the difference is that retail sites are designed specifically for sales, while the main functions of social sites are still shared and connected. Social commerce encourages shoppers and sellers to discuss their online shopping experience in forums and communities and exchange notes. While e-commerce interactions are managed through the seller's website, these interactions can also take place via online chat, which is very useful.

Social commerce can have an emotional value that improves online customer travel. Social commerce, built on social media platforms, allows users to interact with each other and exchange ideas, information, and experiences. Whether you're tapping into your social walls - tapping into e-commerce options or adding call-to-action buttons - you have plenty of options for social commerce.

Social commerce allows users to buy and send gifts, redeem coupons and shop on the platform, making it the most popular form of e-commerce worldwide. The entire shopping experience takes place on social media platforms such as Facebook, Twitter, Instagram, and Pinterest. In some stores, the entire shopping experience happens before the customer leaves the social media site.

Shopify's study shows that Instagram has the highest number of active users and the second-highest percentage of social media users. Instagram is also one of the world's leading social media platforms when it comes to social commerce. Studies have shown that Facebook commerce is not a viable form of social commerce, especially if it is not as popular as other social platforms that users can click on.

There may be some technologies that enable social trade, but the rationale is still social. Social commerce offers the opportunity to bring certain products to certain people who would love them in ways that other forms of commerce cannot. It helps to get people to buy where they buy.

Possible options include brands collaborating with live streaming platforms to launch and sell products and other forms of communication through super apps that communicate through social media.

In short, social commerce is the use of social media and online communities for the sale of goods and services. That's what the funds do, and it's used to buy and sell things based on its reviews in an online community. In short, it is a form of marketing, advertising, and sales in a social environment.

Instagram Reels

Instagram recently introduced a new way to create video content and share it with friends and the community in general. Instagram Reels is a content format that allows users to create 15-second videos and share them with each other via the new Feed Explore page.

Instagram Reels can be created, and accessed from any mobile device such as iPhone, iPad, Android, or Windows Phone.

Instagram reels could also be a way for brands and companies to better understand their Instagram community before getting started.

What's all the hoopla?

"It sounds like a TikTok clone, and a really cheap one, at that."

Well, the case of reels being a TikTok feature clone are debatable, however, Instagram must be learning from the defeat of TikTok's predecessor, Vine. Instagram's parent company, Facebook, watched years ago as the other mega giant, Twitter, purchased and closed the platform. Many cite that Instagram video killed the app.

Obviously, Instagram is attempting to beat TikTok at its own game, and to take users away from the brand.

What's The Downside of All That Money? – The Ugly Side of the Influencer Industry

Social media influencers not only have a lot of followers, but those followers also have confidence in a particular person, and that's a big deal.

If we're looking from a business owner's perspective, you want to authentically present your brand, product, or service to a large audience; a social media influencer may be just the thing for you. You may be interested in what social media influencers are, what they do, and how you can build a relationship with them, but getting started can be difficult. Influencers are a valuable resource for companies that want to expand their reach, so choose the best of them that you want to work with.

When you work with a social media influencer, they develop specific content about your brand and place you at the top of their list.

Find a social media influencer with an established image that works for your brand, who you see as a complement to your product or service, and who has followers who are also members of your target group. You can determine whether you should bring them on or not. For example, if your company produces mountain climbing equipment – you'd need a mountain climbing influencer who just attempted to climb Mount Everest as an extreme example.

The more followers you have, the more likely you are to make money as a social media influencer, but what salary could you expect if you were in their shoes? It depends on how influential they are, how many followers they have, and how powerful they are within your brand. Social media influencers' pay will vary from company to company, as will their power in the companies and the brand(s) they work for.

A good example would be a beauty brand that works with a social media influencer to create a limited-edition product that influencers can promote.

Do Jeffree Star and Shane Dawson and their palette together ring a bell? You know your target group well enough to understand the benefits of your products and services and use them in a way that benefits your customer's business. Brands need to be aware of their audience and appeal to the social-media-savvy generation.

When brands look for potential social media influencers they can work with, they will look for influencer relevance, reach, and retention rates. Forget about the social media marketing strategy beyond the personality of the brand you mention or the content you share. Before you prepare for a new marketing campaign with a customer selected by a social media influencer, it's time to look at other campaigns you've been involved in and that have proven successful in the past. Speaking of Jeffree Star and Shane Dawson – you may not be seeing any new promotional deals for a while for the two of them, with the light on their recent social scandals.

Some social media influencers don't make any money but have a wide range of different jobs, from advertising and marketing to business development. Many of them become actors, models, musicians, or even become famous, and some of these people are commonly known as "social media influencers." These people are experts in tactics that aim to gain influence, followers, and authority by working with more popular people. The most important brand influencers include celebrities, experts, gurus with many followers, professional athletes, and YouTube stars. These individuals don't make the bulk of their income through their social media profiles but instead, use them as a "fame booster shot" to become more visible and respected in their fields.

A social media influencer can also be defined as working in a particular industry and working with followers from within. The definition of a "social media influencer" goes beyond the number of followers you can attract to a social network or website. Still, there are many other things you need to make your influence on social media official. Whether it's a review posted on Yelp or TripAdvisor, you must have had some influence on social media to be an influencer promoting your product, service, or brand.

Buying Followers

Several exciting new technologies have recently come onto the market to enable social media marketers and influencers to increase Instagram followers and follower engagement with just the quick entering of their credit card. You've probably seen or encountered this kind of advertising, and the idea of buying likes and Instagram followers has started to circulate on social media. This may sound tempting to aspiring social media users, but it's not the most effective way to enlarge your Instagram followers.

Don't just rely on buying Instagram followers; see it as an additional way to make your brand and product portfolio more widely known. Investing in a solution is more important than deciding whether to buy an Instagram follower because it brings more than just organic followers.

Before we delve into the basics of succession and gain more followers, we should figure out what it means to follow healthily on social media.

You should focus on getting authentic followers who can interact with your other social media accounts, not just how many people follow your profiles. You may have 10,000 Twitter followers, but you've just opened an Instagram account and a Facebook page, and you're promoting both. You can use the Twitter account to drive followers to the other new pages.

If you opt for social media marketing, your money will likely be spent paying Facebook and Twitter directly to boost your posts and place ads on the authentic followers you already have. However, many companies can't cope with social media marketing and have no problem getting Instagram followers. Again, this makes buying followers a waste of money, but it's much less efficient if you use it to buy fake followers, and Instagram will delete them from your account as soon as they become aware of the problem. Even worse, you could be "shadowbanned" – removed from the algorithm without being notified, rendering your account hard to find.

Instagram tools like the ones mentioned above can help social media marketers dramatically increase their follower count in a short space of time. Still, if you buy fake followers, it is unlikely that your business will benefit from these followers when building a true, organic following on social media. While there are plenty of "Instagram hacks" to get more followers, buying Instagram hacks is something of a retreat and goes against the purpose of social media.

In this respect, if you have more followers, even if they are fake, it can lead to more engagement and engagement with your followers. Right? Wrong.

There are several reasons why you shouldn't buy followers on social media, but here are the main reasons why you should avoid buying followers and stick to building an organic audience. There's no reason to buy Instagram likes, and if you only get five likes on every post, what's that for thousands of Instagram followers? There are so many ways to grow engagement organically to help grow your followers in the right way.

Hiring a Robot

Let's think of an example. You find someone in your interest niche – let's say, travel, and like five pictures, comment on three and hope to get one follower in return.

This could be automated in the past. I did it, and it worked amazingly. This is how I went from 2K to 10K.

The coolest thing is that this is not buying followers. Real people are the ones hitting the follow button because they like you. You can automate a bad profile and won't get any followers since the relevant and interesting content isn't there. Your profile needs to resonate with them. Things have changed, and automation is not possible anymore. However, loads still do it manually; I don't because it's time-intensive, but this way is not bad; in my opinion, you just get their attention, and they decide whether they follow you or not.

They're Usually Depressed

Instagram sensation Essena O'Neill quit social media because she felt a life built on getting "likes" was harmful. This is not the first time we have seen an emotional breakdown by a social media celebrity. Young, privileged digital influencers are now recognizing anxiety and depression symptoms and are raising questions about whether social media can harm our mental health. From Beyonce and Katy Perry to

Rihanna and Meghan Trainor, several celebrities have discussed their feelings of depression and anxiety in emotional and revealing open letters. The trend, or revelation, seems to be growing.

There may be many reasons why social media is associated with increased anxiety and depressive symptoms, but the increased social comparison is strongest. This does not necessarily mean that social media causes these problems, and it is unclear whether media use harms people who are already more depressed or anxious. Most studies have shown that time spent on social media is correlated with depression and anxiety. Still, they have not determined whether depressed and anxious young people spend more time on social media or whether it contributes to their mental health problems. That's right, even those stars you love so much are comparing themselves to the next person up to their proverbial "totem pole."

According to Psychology Today, it can also contribute to eating disorders and self-harming behavior, making it harder for stars to turn off social media for their mental health. It is also important to recognize that dependence on social media makes life stressful. It is not always possible to take a break for a career, family, or various other reasons. Ultimately, it's up to the celebs whether they need time off social media to improve their mental health or not. Celebrities and ordinary people can stay healthy while using it, even if it is not always feasible.

PR and image specialist Majorie Wallens explains that social media makes it easier for celebrities to engage with fans in real-time.

They Edit Their Photos
We all use Photoshop & Lightroom, Lightroom to enhance colors and

brighten photos. Photoshop is used widely to an alternate reality, which I don't agree with. People photoshop bodies, going so far as to change physiques and eye colors. People change locations, skies, mountains, etc. Some people will get disappointed that it is not real.

Sponsorships Don't Always Work Out

A big part of sponsorship is to showcase a business to an audience, and you may have incredible talent doing so, but without that audience there, it isn't possible. However, it is not realistic to expect a big sponsorship deal right away, as you are still working on expanding your audience. For example, you could be approached by a company that is simply not in the market for a podcast sponsorship deal but instead offer a discount code to give out.

Huge web celebrities have an audience, but the problem is that their audiences are generally youngsters – meaning that there have been many occasions where young audience members have been shown inappropriate images or products for someone their age.

For example, Nike Inc.'s recent ad campaign "Just Do It" starring Colin Kaepernick has blown up the Internet, as expected. Since the launch, Nike lit a social media fire with its new "Just Do" campaign featuring Kaepernick, the controversial political quarterback.

While the uproar would make one change his mind, Kaepernick's ad doesn't even mention his role in fueling the recent wave of athlete activism that is on the move. While his Nike-released commercial explicitly mentions protests against police shootings and all things controversial, it has become synonymous with kneeling in protest of police violence against black men and women, making the two almost inseparable. Kaepernick also knelt during the national anthem the past two seasons during a game against the San Francisco 49ers on September 16, 2016, drawing anger from President Trump, which, in all reality, only signal boosted Nike's campaign.

Perhaps the new ad's slogan is, in this sense, a direct response to the recent wave of protests against police violence in the United States. Kaepernick's quote "Believe in something, even if it means sacrificing everything," juxtaposed with a photo of Kaepernick shows that Nike is firmly behind the player and his cause.

If you believe in brands' power and purpose and want polarization and controversy, you can't ignore Nike's Kaepernick ad without provoking controversy, and that's exactly what it does. If you look at the ad, you will see that it is not the product advertised, but the famous Nike logo, which is matched with the company's equally famous slogan. Nike is not controversial for the sake of controversy, they stand for Kaepernick and stand with him against social issues in America. But that doesn't mean Nike is giving money pointlessly to some political statement void.

Colin Kaepernick used his brand and platform to speak up for his community. People cheered loudly and praised Nike for taking up the controversy surrounding the former NFL quarterback and his espoused social positions. By signing, Nike shows that it is part of their brand to take a stand, but they are also listening and demonstrating their commitment to Kaepernick's cause – while still whispering their message of selling shoes in the background.

What makes this campaign so important for Nike and their brand is the direction that sports and culture are taking.

Kaepernick and Nike have been in business together since 2011, and despite the controversy surrounding him, the company has never cut ties with him. Nike was and is the exclusive supplier of NFL jerseys, even though the NFL fined Kaepernick for kneeling during the anthem. Nike has always been the exclusive supplier of NFL uniforms, despite Kaepernick's claim that he was "blackmailed" by the NFL after he kneeled during the anthem.

Colin Kaepernick has been sidelined, established sports culture

Nike chose Kaepernick when every other brand on the planet wouldn't even dare call his name. Still, Kaepernick is someone the brand has invested in and been promoted to the public for years, and he and what he represents are in tune with the progressive audience they want to reach. It takes a lot more than asking Colin Kaepernick to be a spokesman for your brand, even if he's willing and able to be. Nike took a bold step in the Colin Kaepernick campaign by having him believe in its brand, not just its marketing strategy.

Instead of sacrificing everything to Kaepernick, Nike has simply turned him into an extremely well-paid pro. Even people who support Kaepernick as an NFL protester don't like Nike using him for marketing. Sports journalist Zito Madu said the ad dilutes and commercializes Kaepernick's message, suggesting that buying Nike clothing is part of Kaepernick's support.

Politics aside, the truth remains that Nike didn't think twice when they made Colin Kaepernick the face of Nike. Do just that, and you will do great damage to the brand image, not just for Kaepernick, but for the NFL, should a misstep be made.

Is the question – was it a good move or not?

There Are Negative Impacts on Their Own Families

Many parents share pictures and videos of their children on social media, but more live off them. With big brands entering into paid partnerships, more and more companies are looking to make a profit, even off of so-called "family channels."

Children in these families get a raw end of the deal, as sponsored influencer videos empower them, and second, by the influence of their parents.

However, on a day-to-day basis, toy companies should be careful to use their social media presence with the so-called "influencers." The reason children want to become influencers because the world opens up to them, and they like the idea of networking. Still, you know as well as I do that there are villains out there – some as common as the man or woman next door or multi-national conglomerates that only want bottom lines – you've seen all of those Disney stars go off the rails.

Moreover, active social media use is likely to increase parents' intrapersonal empowerment and increase their likelihood of communicating their influencers' impact. Combined, this would suggest that parents' social media engagement can increase their level of comfort, understanding, and trust by enabling social media to function, thereby contributing to the development of their children's self-esteem and social skills. Still, it doesn't work out that way, as studies have shown that parents and children are increasingly spending less time together – especially when there's a social media channel to run! In these cases, the time spent together is likely to produce a new video – not exactly the quality time, reading from a script, and acting out zany skits.

Based on the above research, we expect parents who actively use social media to be more empowered, and to have a more critical view. Overall, parents should be encouraged to actively engage their young children within social media influencers' topic. We expect that there are benefits to actively using social media and empowering themselves more to rely on their community, as it is born of passive use of social media.

If you want to understand better the impact of social influencer marketing on young people, you need to find out which influencers have a strong following among "Gen Z" users. Suppose you're not yet working on an influential marketing campaign, following influences on Facebook, Twitter, Instagram, Pinterest, and other social media platforms to see what percentage of your posts are supported and what products and brands you love. You'll see that target audience.

Many experts are concerned that children could exploit the money they can earn on social media negatively, such as taking part in scams or stumbling across, or even worse, producing inappropriate content.

While mom blogs have raised concerns that children should be protected from their parents publishing intimate and private details of their lives without consent, there are still families lining up around the block to use their children to review toys or play a part in skits. The frontrunner on a YouTube channel that reviews toys, raking in millions, is under seven years old. Internet celebrity JoJo Siwa is actually in her teenage years, despite what her childish character's demeanor would portray.

Child therapist Sascha Kirpalani says parents have a crucial role to play in helping influencer children deal with the impact of fame and social media on their lives. In this regard, we consider it important to understand social media's marketing tactics to prepare young people better to deal with incoming persuasive messages. In summary, we found that parents who are actively involved in social media use are better equipped to increase their self-efficacy, competence, control, and belief while simultaneously communicating the impact of their adolescents' social media use on their mental health.

In normal parental mediation, which includes social media sharing, monitoring children's use of social media, and rules governing their use is likely to positively impact a child's understanding of social media and ads. For example, parents will be offered the opportunity to discuss the media's impact on children and their mental health and the possible negative effects on their health and well-being. Unfortunately, in the case where the entire family is part of a social media brand, there is no defining line.

The great thing about influencer marketing is that social media platforms are changing quickly, and influencers have changed their brands and price points. Recently, a growing number of "influencer families" have taken the opportunity to work with brands and post content on social media. The impact of marketers of public and social responsibility who have implemented influential marketing programs has been enormous, contradicting the widespread view that it is merely a tactic to sell products and can be a force of good; however, that line can sometimes be difficult to distinguish, and we've seen several families go overboard, and in turn, be destroyed by it.

What is Social Influence? (Social Influence and What it Means)
Social Influence is how people change their behavior to fit in with the rest of the social environment (let's say a group).

Some examples are:

-Peer Pressure

-Conformity (where you match someone else's behavior)

-Obedience

-Persuasion

Brands hire us as influences because we have a group (followers) that are likely to conform to our behavior, including our purchasing habits. The more influential people promote something, the more everyone will feel the pressure to buy that product.

The Science of Influencing
Let's reverse for a bit and look at the scientifically studied facts of "influence."

Charismatic Authority
Max Weber's writings on "charismatic authority," for example, conceptualized influence as a socially and culturally constructed phenomenon in 1946. Weber focused on the political and economic circumstances out of which influential leaders arise, arguing that "in

times of psychic, physical, economic, ethical, religious, (or) political distress," leaders who seem to have exceptional qualities tend to become influential – in the case of Max Weber's time, Adolf Hitler.

The People's Choice, in 1948, which reported the results of a study conducted by Paul Lazarsfeld, Bernard Berelson, and Hazel Gaudet during the 1940 election, was an early milestone in sociological understandings of influence. In this study, the authors sought to understand how people made voting decisions, finding that other people's influence was "more frequent and more effective than the mass media." Remember, this was in the 1940's – long before Instagram, computers, and cell phones; this speaks volumes.

Personal Influence

The part played by people in the flow of mass communication, studied in 1955, Katz and Lazarsfeld explicitly outline the two-step flow model, wherein people who act as "opinion leaders" or "influentials" filter information from the mass media to their friends and neighbors. Ordinary people's interactions with these influential people drive some behavior and opinion formation. Drawing on a study of women's decision-making on topics from public affairs to fashion conducted in Decatur, Illinois, Katz and Lazarsfeld argued that people were not "a mass of disconnected individuals hooked up to the media but not to each other," as many believed, but were comprised of "networks of interconnected individuals through which mass communications are channeled."

Cialdini, for example, famously outlined six "weapons of influence" that he deduced from experimental and participant observation research, emphasizing how certain norms that seem to be embedded in most human cultures—such as reciprocity, compliance with 15 authority, and looking to "social proof" (what others are doing) when making certain decisions—can be used to get people to think or behave in certain ways. This work recognizes the increasing sophistication of influence tactics utilized by people and organizations, from salespeople to media organizations.

Giveaway Loops

Loop giveaway contests are currently very popular in the influencer world, and brands are gaining ground. I'll go through just a few reasons why an Instagram loop contest might not be very effective for your growth.

If you're wondering if loop giveaways work, the short answer is yes, but they're pretty thirsty. Each account can win a small prize in a loop competition, and all loop members can participate in a larger prize together. The influencers involved in the loops and giveaways split what they give away and split it across all accounts.

You can use Instagram to host giveaways, or you can come out big and team up with others to create a ribbon gift. If many people participate in the loop, the host can set up separate Instagram accounts for each sweepstake, so there is no need for each sweepstake.

Each brand participating in a loop giveaway must post the same image with the same wording. The images used for each contest should be about the same, so people know the account in the right place.

There is no doubt that giveaway loops attract followers, but it does not guarantee that they are active and can benefit from them.

When you run a loop competition, you cannot control who enters the sweepstakes, and you are unlikely to reach your target audience. That's not to say that taking part in loop raffles to increase your following can hurt. If you're hoping for long-term loyal followers, you are then grinding, and freebies aren't your best choice. There are many examples of those who have made loops or giveaways and gained 100k followers with engagement that didn't fit.

The biggest kicker is that the success rate of a loop competition (or any other competition) will vary depending on the way it is set up. This could either send the organizer to the cleaners or running smiling to the bank with their new follower list.

Whenever you make an Instagram Loop Giveaway, a large proportion of the followers you gain will no longer follow after the giveaway. On top of this, people are less likely to participate in a loop competition to track multiple new accounts. It seems that every account that enters a loop draw loses hundreds of followers once it is over, but many still lose some of their previous draws. Many grow by getting sucked into a giveaway, losing some followers, and then running another giveaway to start a new cycle—a constant up-down effect.

Other times, however, participants in a loop competition may be persons on the list of participants. It is set up by the third-party provider - the hosting of the loop competition or the sweepstakes. Often, third-party loops and giveaway hosts have their own social media accounts.

If you plan to coordinate a loop contest, make sure you buy the prize before securing the entrants and running the sweepstakes. In loop raffles, you need to enter your sponsor's contribution and then compare the image with the next party's tags in the loop. This is a great idea if the influencer in your loop can't offer your product or if you want an expensive reward for your freebies.

Instagram's terms and conditions include a page dedicated to the state of participation in a loop competition that does not violate any rules in any way. First, many loop raffles require you to pay a fee to a third party who organizes the raffle and shares the prize's cost with the other influencers involved. The only major expense you are likely to have during a loop draw would be your sweepstake, but even that is a small amount, as you will share the costs among yourself as the host. If you have to buy a prize yourself for a raffle, the purchase price will often be quite high to get something worth entering the loop for.

Instagram Pods

If you're new to Instagram marketing, this may be the first time you've heard of Instagram Comment Engagement Pods, but there's a lot more to it than how to join an Instagram Pod. An Instagram Engagement Pod is a small group of people who gather in a pod where users show the rest of the group that they have just posted a photo or video to Instagram. Think like Facebook groups!

Typical Instagram pods (also known as comment pods or engagement pods) work in a similar niche and with a similar audience. Instagram Pods consists of people willing to engage with Instagram's content to improve posts in users' feeds. Usually bloggers, writers, artists, designers, photographers, and other social media professionals are associated together.

Technically, an Instagram pod is a group of up to 30 Instagrammers who coordinate in group chats to comment on each other's posts. Instagram pods are groups of people who agree to like, comment on, or like each other's posts, but not necessarily in a direct way. An Instagram Pod is when people join in group chats or forums where users tell the rest of the group that they have just posted a photo or video to Instagram.

The second type of Instagram Engagement Pod is the Instagram Group DM, which follows a slightly different structure described below. Instagram users use DM to inform each other about their new Instagram posts, and other members of their Instagram group must deal with the content within a certain period.

The M.O. of an Instagram Pod is pretty simple: Every time someone in your pod posts a new Twitter post or posts content to Instagram, the pod shares it with the group. Each pod member can support others by liking and commenting on every post sent to that group, but Instagram pods communicate with each other via Instagram DM.

On top of that, there's something to be said for the effort that goes into being part of an Instagram engagement pod. If you prefer not to spend too much time in the app and just like to post about your work from time to time, you will find it hard to keep up with Instagram Pod Groups. Not to mention that you can take it to the next level with the help of other Instagram pods and groups, but you have to want to work with them.

Social Media Isn't Healthy (The Effects of Social Media on Mental Health)

Social media can not only make us unhappy, but it is also linked to mental health problems, including anxiety, depression, and suicide. We dominate our news programs and contribute to rising rates of depression, anxiety, and suicide in the United States and around the world with it.

Research into the effects of social media on the brain has led to scientific findings on mental illness. Much of this research focuses on the relationship between social media and mental health, including depression and anxiety. Social media use and health-related outcomes such as depression, anxiety, and suicide could go both ways.

While social media itself may not be responsible for mental health problems, it can be a vehicle for distress if handled too carefully. Social media has been shown to cause discontent, but it is not the only cause of mental illness in adolescents and young adults. In particular, social media can hurt young people who suffer from or are vulnerable, such as bullying.

Awareness of the impact of spending time on social media and considering the impact on mental health is the first step to protecting mental health. With these tips, you can create healthy social media habits that balance your life, protect your mental health, and ensure you use them as a positive force, not a negative force.

It's hard to name an app or service that does nothing to harm mental health, although some studies have cited Instagram as a trigger for anxiety and depression. Instagram reports that it is responsible for up to 20% of all social media use and recently began to hide the number to reduce users' pressure.

We know that social media and mental health have a controversial relationship. We understand why they suggest and know deep down that we would all be better off if we could still free ourselves from the grip of these media platforms. We all know it can help to connect with the world around us. Still, every time we use it, research finds that too much can harm our mental health.

Social media has several positive characteristics, but those benefits are drowned out when social media usage becomes mindless.

Young people, who generally use social media more than the general population, benefit from this digital phenomenon's connectivity and positive impact. Despite this networking and the positive effects, it has also been associated with mental health problems. Recent research on depression and social media suggests that teenagers who consume it for more than three hours a day are at higher risk of developing mental illness than those who do not. According to a recent study in Psychological Science, teenagers who have used social media for less than two hours a day for the past two years are more likely to internalize negative feelings such as anxiety and depression than deal with them.

Addicted (The Signs of Social Media Addiction)

More and more people are talking about addiction to social media, and there are many reasons people consider it one of the most common mental health problems in the US. There is even a new study circulating, "Social Media Addictions After the Fact." Some researchers argue that addiction behaviors to social media may overlap with those that occur in addictive behaviors that remain hidden from others, such as the desire to experience a sense of escapism.

If all of this seems relevant to you, it may be time to put down your phone, hide your tablet or laptop and start being truly social. If you or someone close struggles with an addiction to social media and has a complete inability to separate from it, it may be time to get some help.

If you are worried about your social media addiction, making an addiction therapist appointment is a good start. A mental health patient can help you determine whether you really have a social media addiction or just enjoy using it. There is no shame in having a problem with your phone, tablet, laptop, computer, or other electronic device and seeking professional help.

Knowing that the signs of a social media addiction are accompanied by time on the page, you can tell exactly whether the addiction is present or not. Social media can be an addiction, but it can also be considered a habit disorder, so you can see signs from what you do throughout the day.

What worries me most is that addiction to social media is often exacerbated by other addictive substances rarely discussed, such as alcohol and drug addiction. Many doctors see a strong correlation between addiction and other mental health problems. Still, there is more to determining whether someone is a "social media addict" and more evidence of a social media addiction than all of these.

And the symptoms of depression and low self-esteem that accompany social media addiction are not unique to viewers. Another factor that continues the addiction to social media is that the brain's reward centers are most active when people talk to other people.

Social media addicts rely on them to kill time, have entertainment, and satisfy their need for social interaction with friends and family members.

Social media addiction is not a formal clinical diagnosis, but most experts agree that social media addiction is a serious problem and falls under behavioral addiction. It is fair to say that many people spend far too much time on social media, describing themselves as "obsessed" but not addicted. Although social media is more addictive than alcohol and cigarettes, there are no formal, clinical diagnoses that could label a person a "social media addict." Although a relatively small number of people are diagnosed as addicted, social media's negative effects are obvious enough to be considered clinical addiction, according to the National Institute on Drug Abuse (NIDA).

Like other addictions, mobile phones' use leads to an increase in the brain's chemical dopamine, which temporarily makes us feel good and makes us want more. The neurotransmitter dopamine is at the heart of addiction - cravings for phones, for everything. To effectively break down dependence on smartphones, we need to separate the things responsible for dopamine release. This tells us that there are changes in the brain and that it can be a game of chicken and egg, but in this case, with a smartphone.

New research suggests that dependence on devices and substances like alcohol and drugs affects the brain as cardiovascular diseases such as heart disease and diabetes. Just as cardiovascular disease damages the heart and changes its function, addiction alters our brain and impairs its functions.

A study on mindfulness training showed increased cognitive performance, and cognitive-behavioral therapy (CBT) was found to restructure the brain. In contrast, the same study examined the brains of phone-dependent users. It has been shown that the same areas of our brains are damaged by smartphone addiction. Addiction causes changes in cells' function and signaling, including synapses, the molecular learning machine.

The researchers believe the relationship between the two substances could provide clues to addiction, particularly smartphone addiction. The amount of both chemicals in the study participants clearly showed that the brain is altered with smartphone addiction. Smartphone addiction is a major cause of mental health problems such as depression and anxiety.

09: Brand Activism

"A meaning behind the message."

What is Brand Activism?

Brand activism, also known as Corporate Social Responsibility (CSR), is when a company tries to have a positive impact on a cause that aligns with its mission. It is the effort your brand makes to promote the values of your brand in relation to its mission. In addition, the definition of "brand activism" refers to situations where companies share an idea that is typically consistent with the defined corporate value.

If you think the topic is right for your brand and decide it is "right" for the company and how you want to position yourself, you need to encourage your efforts. It is not about jumping on the bandwagon of brand activism by following the news, but it has to be part of the message that the brand wants to create. This means recognizing that brand activism is not a PR stunt or marketing opportunity but an opportunity to find out how your organization can contribute to the greater good.

Where brand activism is a strategy, content marketing is how the brand communicates its attitude to these activities. Marketing brand activism can be as simple as shedding light on food inequality or sponsoring a local artist who paints a mural on climate change. Unlike corporate social responsibility efforts that focus on making the company's core product or activities more socially responsible, brand activism deals with social, environmental, and human issues that are not directly related to the company's core product business.

As a quick Google search shows, it is important to consider the different verticals of brand activism because depending on the actions and core values of a company, one form of brand activism may not fit into the other. Traditional activism aims for meaningful change, while brand activism uses social issues that are relevant to consumers. However, an evolving understanding suggests that value-driven brands that have the resources to mobilize and act have a better chance of gaining influence and reaping the rewards through brand activists. To make brand activism financially sustainable, it is vital that the causes you need to associate with your brand are closely linked to your commercial agenda.

It has the added benefit of positively influencing the outcome of a business, and it has taken CSR to a whole new level, with brands becoming active as visible entities that point the way to its cause. Brand activism brings the social values, beliefs, and causes of a company to life in a way that creates positive changes in the world. It does not generate the same public awareness as other forms of CSR, but it does have its own added value in positively influencing business results.

How to Generate Brand Activism

It is important to consider brand activism because the responses reflect the motives and moral behavior of the company's brand. Companies have been creating profiles of corporate social responsibility for decades, but "brand activism" or "cause marketing" represent something completely different. While corporate "social responsibility" efforts focus on positively impacting the lives of their employees, customers, and families, "brand activism" addresses social, environmental, and human issues that are not directly related to the company's core products and operations. For brands, activism is about leveraging resources and expertise to solve the social problems of the communities they serve.

To make the world a better place, brand activism can also have a positive impact on a company's bottom line. Supporting brand activists is about donating a portion of your sales to a particular group or organization by sharing why you support those sales. Moreover, engaging in "brand activism" can also have the advantage of linking consumers' purchases from the company with supporting their own values. It starts to turn into a win-win.

For brand activism to be financially sustainable, it is crucial that the causes you associate with your brand are intricately linked to your commercial agenda. One can imagine setting up a social media account where one can support a cause through donations or by helping to raise awareness of the cause.

If you know your target customers, take low risks and use the right digital channels to develop the "right" strategy for brand activism, you will create content that attracts customers who share the same values as your company's brand. Brand activism will help you raise awareness of your brand and the causes you support, as well as more revenue. It can also create an opportunity to turn your customers into brand ambassadors.

By applying brand activism, a company demonstrates its commitment to the community it serves and the economic, social, and environmental issues that enable it to build a value-based relationship with customers and stakeholders. Brands that use brand activism develop a more natural relationship of trust because consumers are more likely to support campaigns that help a cause they believe in. Consumers are less surprised when brands choose activism, and brands are also less surprised when they receive backlash for certain statements. Most companies that engage in brand activism conclude that the loyalty that results outweighs any distaste for those who disagree.

Brand activism has the added advantage of positively influencing the outcome of a company, but it does not generate the same public awareness as other forms of social activism. Brand activism can use the influence of companies to raise awareness of critical issues, which in turn has the marketing benefit of aligning itself with these issues. Companies need to analyze their own core values and remain authentic to have a real impact on the audience. Others are affected by the impact of activism when it is directly consistent with their digital strategy.

This means recognizing that brand activism is not a PR stunt or marketing opportunity but an opportunity to find out how your organization can contribute to the greater good. To be successful, brands must understand that sincerity and consistency must underlie all efforts they make to harness the power of brand activism. The PR department must invest heavily in brand image campaigns that give consumers a passionate sense of their brand so that their commitment to a brand does not negatively affect their intention to participate in a boycott. It is not about jumping on the bandwagon of brand activism by following the news but rather about the message the brand wants to create.

What Does Brand Activism Do?

Brand activism is when a company tries to have a positive impact on the lives of its customers and the world at large. In a survey by the World Media Group, leading media brands such as ABC, CBS, NBC, and Fox cited "brand activism" as the most important way for brands to connect with consumers on import issues. It's out there, and you've likely seen or even participated in it.

As a quick Google search shows, it is important to consider the different verticals of brand activism because depending on the actions and core values of one company, one form of "brand activism" may not fit the other. There are many ways to engage in brand activism, and it can be as simple as a social media campaign or as complex as a lobbying campaign. Think support for the LGBTQ community with rainbow products during "Pride Month" or lobbying government entities for stronger gun control laws.

Recognizing that brand activism is not a PR stunt or marketing opportunity, but an opportunity to find out how your organization can contribute to the greater good is important, mainly for the fact that if customers discover your activism is indeed a stunt, be prepared for the fallout.

Perhaps the most important thing to consider when considering a brand's purpose and ideas for "brand activism" is to make sure, first and foremost, that everything your brand does is consistent with what you want to say.

Also, it is crucial to keep an eye on the impact of brand activism on consumer activism. For brand activists to be financially sustainable, the causes that you associate with your brand are of crucial importance, closely linked to your commercial agenda.

In addition, "brand activism" can make the world a better place and have a positive impact on your company's bottom line. Moreover, engaging in brand activism can also have the benefit of connecting consumers to your business with the support of their own values.

While brand activism is on the rise, social benefits and targeted campaigns with brand messages do not guarantee successful results.

Supporting "brand activism" is as simple as donating some of your sales to a particular group or organization while also explaining why you support it. Brand activism takes CSR to the next level as brands become active as visible entities that lead the way for their cause. It brings to life the social values, beliefs, and causes of a company in a way that creates positive change in the world. Brand activism has developed as a value-driven agenda for companies that care about the future of society, the planet, and health.

Those who participate in brand activism use a larger platform for good and show consumers that the brand is there for them, respects them, and wants to help make the world a better place. Brands that use brand activists develop a more natural relationship of trust, as consumers are more likely to support campaigns that help the causes they believe in.

Where brand activism is a strategy, content marketing is how a brand communicates its attitude and activities. Social media is an effective platform for brand activists because it is a place to share brand personalities and is often one of the first platforms consumers discover. Don't confuse the two!

Examples of Brand Activism

Two notable examples of brand activism have emerged during the pandemic, the mask-wearing campaign in the United States and the campaign against the Ebola virus in Africa; but these aren't the traditional sense campaigns you're looking for.

Ben & Jerry's has made its activism accessible to the public through content marketing, from a page on its website that provides access to its blog posts that address issues to the reasons it makes flavors, social media and PR initiatives.

To position yourself as a truly socially conscious activist, it is critical for consumers to believe that your brand believes authentically and passionately in the causes it supports, rather than just jumping on a bandwagon. Brands that use brand activism can build a more natural relationship of trust, as consumers are more likely to support campaigns that support the cause they believe in. Initiatives for brand activism begin with the ability of a brand to be considered as a "brand in its own right."

The company feels strongly about the cause of advocacy, and attempts at brand activism reflect a sincere belief that the issue is relevant to the brand, even if people quickly recognize false associations. Moreover, brand activation can also create a more natural relationship with consumers by getting them to combine buying from a company with supporting their own values. Comprehensive brand activists can donate a portion of their sales to a specific group or organization without having to share why they support the sale.

Experiential brand activism can be realized through experiential values, in addition to many other approaches that directly influence people and culture. This ice cream company has mastered this.

10: Starting Your Own Magazine/eBook

"Magazines are the most effective way to create tons of branded content on all platforms!"

How to Start an Online Magazine

If you are thinking about starting an online magazine or publication, here is an exciting story - you may not have thought about how to make money from it when you started it, but you should identify some potential sources of funding as early as possible because it's possible to bring in realistic income from such ventures.

Take a Look Around

To make the most of it and stay ahead of the competition, I suggest that you study and spy on their most popular online magazines and try to do some research about them. What's their niche? How large is their audience? Often, publications will share their media kits – these media kits will allow you to take a look at readership statistics, indicating the interest level and how much competition they'll be putting up to your new publication.

Got a Site?

A website is essential for any magazine, and there are a few ways to set one up, but I have seen many good ideas about it in the world of online magazines.

Building the right website is crucial to fulfilling your dream of starting your own online magazine. If you start your publication as a separate business, you'll also need to consider monetization options so that you can focus your efforts on expanding the publication but remember that starting a magazine can be a full-time job, even if you start small.

There is no doubt that there must be a way to turn your website into a revenue stream, whether you make money from advertising, subscriptions, or e-commerce.

Got a Plan?

Creating a business plan for your magazine is a good step, even if you don't plan to make it your business later on. It should include and outline how you intend to run the magazine, publishing business, income generation ideas, and if you'll need staff such as photographers, writers, or distribution agents.

The bottom line is that if you want to build, create, launch, and operate an effective and successful online magazine or website, you need to build a team that believes in your vision and purpose.

Let's Talk Advertising

If you intend to set up a magazine or publishing business from the city where you are active to become a national or international magazine, you do not need to spend money on advertising and promoting your brand.

The best way to do this is to start with just one revenue stream and then introduce more as your online magazine builds traffic.

Getting Started

Once you have signed up for a WordPress.com account, the next step is to select a professionally designed online magazine. Just like an e-book, your digital magazine must have a striking cover that looks like a magazine cover. See if you can mimic the cover elements to make it feel like a magazine for your target audience.

If you own a small business and want your magazine to help increase your business's revenue, you need to design a magazine that has an impact on your readers. An online magazine is beautifully designed to appeal to your target audience and can help you establish yourself as a thought leader in your field, offer value to the audience, and make money for the business.

Why Start an Online Magazine?

A digital magazine is a powerful way to communicate your brand in a robust way, an extension of the website. The online magazine brings your marketing to life, reaching the consumer on their level.

Before you start publishing your online magazine, you need to do proper market research. To ensure that the digital magazine is read, gather information about your target readers before selecting the subject matter. To reflect the demographic development of the readership and to capture alternative terms, make sure the word "magazine" is utilized in Search Engine Optimization.

If you are planning to start an online magazine, it may be important to understand the types of activities that are required for development and marketing. Before you create any kind of magazine, you need to know and understand how to make money from it, so make sure you choose your target audience and topics wisely. When you launch your online magazines, you may not be able to change direction, and that makes it difficult for you to choose wisely for your target audience, or topic.

When you start an online magazine that accepts articles written by real people (as opposed to authors), you don't have to worry so much about writing.

Another way to monetize your online magazine is to sponsor huge distribution channels, such as social media, where you pay for sponsored posts to create content with a particular product, brand, or person.

People are encouraged to choose magazines because it is now easy to gain a wider readership through the Internet, and it costs little or nothing to publish them. The ability to produce digital online magazines has opened up the digital publishing space by enabling virtually anyone to create, publish, disseminate and reach a broad readership. Running your own online newspaper or publication has a huge advantage, as it makes it easier to interact with your readers.

When you are considering setting up an online magazine, you need to be aware of the area you are going to cover and really understand who you are talking to as an audience and what they want. You really want to think deeply about your distribution strategy and plan for the distribution of your magazine.

The next step in launching an online magazine is to make sure you create an editorial product that has all the attributes of a large magazine. Ready-to-buy magazine templates to help you develop your digital magazines; PDFs of your magazine, which your creators can upload online for free, should be quickly uploaded and converted into an interactive online magazine. Those who cannot afford a designer can edit their own magazines and publish them on their website.

Why Invest in Digital Publications?

If you're wondering why you should put your time and effort into monetizing your digital content, then just pick some of the world's most accomplished digital publishers who are focused on today's and tomorrow's financial success, and bam, you have your answer.

More sensitive audience data is the new frontier in digital journalism, enabling publishers to produce personalized, high-quality content with the frequency and format that readers want.

Interactivity in your content is critical to the success of digital publishing, as it encourages new readers and makes your work memorable while providing great value to your readers. Encouraging people to share and enjoy your work is a key element of a successful digital publishing business model and an important part of your marketing strategy.

There is a new audience waiting to read, share and respond to your content, and by using digital publishing services, you will be tapping into new audiences that you might not otherwise have found.

In niche markets, where publishers are willing to invest in digital subscriptions, this can prove a lucrative and predictable source of revenue. In a niche market where publishers are willing to invest in digital subscriptions, it can prove a valuable and reliable source of revenue for publishers.

For print publications, one of the fastest and easiest ways to make money from digital editions is to include them in the subscriptions you offer. Even if you invest in a specific app for your publication, producing a digital journal is cheaper than printing and shipping a physical journal. If you are wondering why you designed the digital edition of your magazine in this way, there are many reasons. Deep insights are the key to a better publishing strategy, so why not prioritize more publications?

There is a large audience for online publications, and digital publications can allow readers with different visual abilities access. You can embed in your digital publication the possibility to offer your customers something that you cannot expect in a paper edition - a printed publication.

One of the main reasons why many publishers and entrepreneurs are going digital is the way they can increase their reach, and this is one way to increase the reach of their publications.

One of the advantages of digital publishing is that e-publications are winning the battle against print and digital journals. Online advertising in the media is much cheaper than the latter, and that is precisely why more publishers are choosing to sell ad space to digital publications rather than print it - publications only. Digital publications reach a wider audience, are faster, and tend to increase the quotation rate compared to a print publication.

While the majority of a printed newspaper's profits may come from ad and subscription sales, digital publishers have more options. Advertising is a significant source of revenue, but it is not as lucrative as subscriptions.

To stay in the digital publishing game, you need to invest in your online presence, be present where your target readers are. This aspect makes digital publications a very attractive business, especially at a time when research results can be dated very quickly before they are actually published. You have a wealth of quantifiable data about your target audience, which allows you to make quick changes to engage your readers.

Why You Should Create A Company Magazine

Here's something to help you get the idea of a company magazine going, whether you're creating a business magazine, website, online magazine, or even an extension of your own business website.

In addition to presenting your products and services, designing a magazine for your company allows you to share the latest news, ideas, and business with your readers.

Be prepared to offer charter rates to attract advertisers who want your magazine, which will help the magazine's look once it hits the market and will prove invaluable in its development. Whether you like it or not, to compete with big magazines, you have to become the competition in the market, and they don't like you when you compete against them.

If you have already produced a small print edition of your company magazines, such as a monthly or quarterly one, it may be time to think about expanding by launching an online magazine. If your goal is to make money from your magazine, you will have many different monetization models at your disposal. Even if you launch a magazine for your business, even if you start small, you still need to consider your monetization options so that your efforts can be focused on growing the publication.

When it comes to launching your own digital magazine, the most important thing is to explore different revenue models for your magazine. You need to decide who the publication is for, how you want to make money, and set a budget for the launch and administration costs of the magazine. Once you decide why you want to create a business magazine, you can work on making your plans happen.

If you are an online publisher looking to build a magazine as a business, you need to invest in good web and magazine design. Most successful digital magazines have websites where people can find out what the magazine is all about. If you are not a design professional, make sure you acquire the design, look and feel of your magazine. In addition, some magazine software offers layout and design tools that ensure that your magazines are sharp. You can also create a website similar to a print magazine but with a much more user-friendly interface.

If you own a small business and want your magazine to help increase your business's revenue, you need to design a magazine that influences your readers. Developing a clear vision of what the current magazine will look like helps you communicate your ideas to potential advertisers and investors. Even if the magazine is only part of your business, the content you publish will lead your target audience back to your business page and the products you offer.

If you have the perfect design and layout for your business magazine, the next thing you need to do is find a reliable printing house. If you can't afford a designer, buy a ready-made magazine template that helps you develop a digital magazine. Once you can secure a free or low-cost resource to produce your magazine for free, you could be able to publish the first issue of your magazines in just a few months.

For this type of magazine to be worth it, you shouldn't expect a return until there's a greater commitment, as Airbnb did with its magazine.

In short, publishing a print magazine is a safe and fast way to help increase your business's sales. If you plan to print a journal as a business, you must start your research first. To create these types of journals, you need to understand the business model and the types of activities required to develop and market an online magazine.

If you want to expand your network of magazine writers, there are a handful of ways to do so. In some niches, it will be of enormous benefit to your magazine if leaders and influencers from your field appear in the magazine. The e-newsletter you publish to promote it may also be a separate profit center if you offer products or services that complement the theme of the magazines.

Why Employee Updates are So Important

The role of the human resources department in a company affects all aspects of the business, as it supports employees as the most important company asset. The HR Department keeps the employees on the ground to maintain job satisfaction and commitment, and even to maintain a positive working environment.

Employees benefit from better communication and more conscious work, and 85% of employees say they are most motivated when management and leadership regularly report on company news. The most effective way to keep them informed and work as a cohesive team is through regular staff meetings. Employees may bring an agenda item or template to the meeting that provides information about the company's current business status, such as the latest news and updates, as well as an overview of current events. Managers who take the time to digest and respond to status updates do important work for their employees.

With regular updates, you can monitor the workload of your direct reports without waiting for employees to be so overwhelmed that they come to you in a crisis. While an employee's status update can take just ten minutes a week, it can make a profound difference in the working environment. While it may not be the most enjoyable part of team leadership, regular review of your employees' work can have a huge impact on their morale and overall productivity. Providing and receiving feedback about your employee's work is not only knowing what is going on but also evaluating your team's performance.

This engagement can mean asking thoughtful questions about events, important news, and updates posted on the company's intranet or sharing what your team is working on with the rest of your organization. An employee meeting is a great opportunity to talk to multiple employees to share important information about company news or updates. Unless a major change is announced or communicated, a company meeting can also be a good opportunity to keep employees and other executives informed of announcements and updates.

By regularly updating their status, managers ask their employees to think about the week ahead, their goals, and their progress. Daily or weekly check-ins are a great opportunity for managers to connect with their team members, identify potential issues early on and adapt to changes and updates accordingly.

Employee manuals can become an important tool in the event of a dispute, and if they are not updated to reflect necessary changes over the years, they can expose your business to the risk of litigation. Done right, current employee manuals provide added value for your organization and employees. Updating the policy regularly provides an opportunity to hand over a new company handbook and have employees sign a confirmation of their contributions. As your business grows and regulations evolve, it is equally important to maintain these documents and ensure that they are not outdated. Although there is a lot of legal jargon that needs to be included in a work manual, it is important that you can formulate the policy in a way that employees understand. Set clear expectations of your employees by also setting out your legal obligations and defining their rights.

Reaching Out to Bloggers in Your Niche

You should always be looking for ways to find influencers in your niche and increase your revenue. We look at the specifics of influencer marketing strategies and their potential impact on your business. To find an influencer that is shared with your target audience, choose a platform such as Facebook, Twitter, Instagram, Pinterest, LinkedIn, or Google + and enter the name of the person you are looking for. Your search for influencers is quick and easy, and you will never question how you can identify a social media influencer on any platform.

If one of these lists covers your niche, you could use that list to determine which influencers in your niche could approach you. Make sure you use this method to find social media influencers and look for a professional to help you find influences that are interested in what you are working on.

Look for influencers who already work with similar brands and who are likely to work with you, and find out if they're promoting your competitors. You need to identify social media influencers who are considered experts in your niche, people who fit your budget, work for a benefit other than money, and are interested in promoting your product. Look for an influencer marketing platform that helps you seek and hire influencers and determine whether they are right for your brand or business. One of them is Buzz Sumo, which allows you to find influencers in every niche to promote content.

A quick scan of your competitor's Instagram accounts can help you find influencers relevant to your niches. For example, if you want to find social media influencers promoting your newly launched cosmetics products, sort by brand to determine which are the most popular social media influencers for your specific niche, such as beauty, health, fashion, and fitness.

You can also hire an influencer marketing agency to find influencers willing to share and link your content.

Once you've found an influencer who works in your niche, the next thing you want to do is find out if you have the right audience or not.

Why Collab with Topic Experts?

Nowadays, collaboration network applications allow you to seek advice from colleagues and professionals from all over the world. To develop your business and build professional connections, collaboration networks offer a wealth of benefits and are a great idea for start-ups, but is that the only reason you should look to them as a resource?

Consider working with an industry influencer who has complementary insights that can build on the content you've already shared. Introducing yourself to the community of experts you work with is a great way to add value to your brand. These influencers are not only aimed at your satisfied target group, but they also have experiences that are worth sharing with you.

How Do I Reel Them In?

Blogging is also an efficient way to network, but it's up to the influencers in your niche. An influencer who already writes about your industry is more likely to share written content about you, just as a popular video creator in your industry is likely to share video content.

Make an effort to find and answer questions on issues that affect your niches. It will help strengthen your authority by offering value. There are plenty of avenues to do this, from Quora to niche interest sites.

Simultaneously, it helps you attract the attention of more prominent influencers in your niche and even opens the door to working with them. This is where the concept of paid advertisements, gifts, and active outreach comes into play.

If you want an influencer to work with you, you need to show them that working together is mutually beneficial. If you have had successful collaborations with bloggers and social media influencers, use these experiences as collateral and let them know how useful this proposal could be. Leave no thought left unturned!

11: Handle That Calendar!

"365 days a year!"

Once you have decided on your social media platforms, you will need to create your own content. The content you create needs to be appropriate to meet your overall goals and your audience; this will ensure that your branding is appropriately updated along with your marketing campaign deadlines.

The type of content and the tone of the content should be appropriate. It should go without saying that it needs to be of a high-quality; do not use pixelated images and do not do bad editing.

Content Scheduling and A Content Calendar

A content calendar is a valuable way to organize your business; there is no one template, but whatever works for you and your needs. Have different sections or color codes for different media and edit until it fits your needs. Do not forget to set aside time to analyze data and reply to comments.

You can schedule posts in advance once you have completed the content to post at an appropriate time for your audience to encourage maximum engagement.

Plan your content in advance, including, and especially, seasonal posts. Planning in advance means you can dedicate your time to the data more important things than stressing to rush out the post or campaign. It would lead to higher quality content and, subsequently, better results. It will also help you better strategize and determine which posts are more successful.

Creating a content calendar is not only a way to plan it but also a way to measure and track your progress to optimize and improve in the future.

Patterns

Eventually, you will be getting into a posting pattern; you will have a kind of content that your audience will begin to expect from you. You should break it up every few posts to try something a little different but definitely try to have a pattern. This will also help with your analytics because it will be easy to see which kind of posts are the most effective, your regular tried and tested content, or newer, more experimental things.

Frequency

You need to decide how often to post, because there are many different factors involved in this process. Different platforms will require different times of posting and different frequencies. However, you should always make it seem as if you are online and available even if you are not. You do not want to come across as a brand that only checks your post once a week and is not available to deal with consumer needs.

Replying

Replying is not content creation, I hear you ask? Perhaps not, but it is a huge value added to a business and needs to be prioritized.

People expect fast replies from businesses. Many people would be more willing to leave a bad review over a bad customer service experience over a suboptimal product. People would rather have an easy way to reply to comments or get in touch with businesses, rather than write an email or ring a number—it is often considered outdated. Having live chats or a social media page that people can contact and get a quick reply is an essential part. You could include an FAQ page or a robot preprogrammed with questions.

Collaboration

Electing to collaborate with another brand is another fantastic way to grow your audience. There are different kinds of collaborations; including partnerships, cross-promotions, content placements, and general collaborations. The time frame on these vary, and some will be more of an investment than others. Collaborating is a way to create new and exciting content, as well as grow your audience.

Recap: The Crucial Difference: Advertising Vs. Marketing

"Know the difference."

As anyone who has worked in the area will tell you, there are explicit differences between advertising and marketing; however, the lines often get blurred. Advertising is a kind of marketing, but that is not all there is to it.

Advertising comes under the umbrella term of marketing. Marketing is much broader and is the combination of all relevant elements in the area.

Definitions also vary, and there is no one fixed answer; however, marketing is more inclusive and comprehensive of different business areas. Whereas advertising may refer specifically to campaigns.

While the difference is not necessarily important in all circumstances, it is still something that you should be aware of. Something that is more explicitly "advertising" may be more likely to be ignored or suppressed by your audience, as opposed to something that comes across as more natural. Often this has to do with branding.

When scrolling through your social media feeds, chances are, you have seen posts labeled with #ad or #sponsored. This is a kind of advertising that falls under the broader marketing strategy. These things are very obviously labeled as advertising, and therefore consumers view them differently from other posts in their feeds. That is, they know that it is clearly trying to sell them on the product. Which, of course, is an important part of marketing, but they should not be the only kinds.

Although many influencers have built brands and lifestyles from advertising products, their power truly comes from their brand. Posting sponsored post after sponsored post would be nothing if they did not build up an audience and brand.

Psychology of social media

As many people know, a big part of marketing is understanding consumers' psychological patterns and determining what makes them act. To complement this, social media was designed to make us spend as much time as possible on the platform. Social media is addictive to many people, and many of us love refreshing our pages to see what new content is there waiting for us. This means that your content needs to be of high quality to light up a consumer's eyes (and screens!), cause them to double-tap and engage meaningfully with your content.

In essence, a good social marketing strategy will understand consumers psychologically and compare this with the psychological underpinnings of each social media platform to create a powerful marketing strategy that uses consumers' patterns and thoughts to get them to act.

Reach

Organic reach and algorithms can challenge brands and businesses. The algorithms are ever-changing and sometimes seem to preference or block posts for no real reason. Often, you are at the mercy of the algorithms. A way to beat this is to have good engagement. Different kinds of engagement and interactions will rank differently. For example, saving or sharing is better than liking. To combat this, try and include competitions or posts that require a direct call to action that people are likely to send the post on to others.

Search engine optimization (SEO)

Optimizing your search engines' content is another fantastic way to assist with your audience and reach new people. It will rank your post higher compared to others. A fun example is that whenever you look up the phrase "social media marketing" regardless of the other search words afterward, you will likely still get results from the same few websites because they have excellent SEO.

Paid content

You may have to add paid posts to your marketing strategy. While these are obviously marketing, there are benefits to doing so. It will place your business in front of new future customers and provide new opportunities for your brand. Checking the analytics and return on your investment is essential to tracking how productive your paid content is.

Avoiding Burnout

Taking a break from work is crucial for digital marketers to stay motivated and produce their best work. Creating a work environment that prevents burnout and promotes healthy work - Life Balance for your digital marketing team is crucial to having a great team, and you know what great teams create – great content!

The quality of your work can be affected by burnout, so you should take breaks to prevent this. Find team members who perform certain tasks that you may avoid and seek advice on how to avoid the negative side effects of burnouts such as depression and anxiety – not good for someone like you who needs to stay on the go.

The creators who can prevent burnout are those who excel in time management, know how to focus on one project after another, and how important it is to build a quality team around them. They are hungry for learning and enthusiastic about creating content, but if they are not careful, they may suffer from doing too much work without proving that they have what it takes to succeed.

Ultimately, the easiest way to prevent burnout in content creation is to delegate it to someone else. If you delegate properly, you can avoid burnouts in the area of digital branding and let your company grow faster and more efficiently.

Create a content marketing calendar that helps you plan a realistic timeline for your content and keep you up to date to get great content. Providing staff with content creation and distribution is useful because it is a simple, highly effective, and a cost-effective technique that increases content efforts and maximizes reach. It is also useful if it is part of your company's overall marketing strategy.

Protecting Yourself (Your Copyright)

The Copyright Act provides that using a copyrighted work for teaching (including multiple copies) does not constitute an infringement of copyright. Fair use and public domain are two aspects of copyright law that many organizations use to use copyrighted material.

The doctrine of fair use is an exception to the Copyright Act, which allows a copyrighted work to be used in certain limited circumstances by seeking its author's permission. In essence, fair use is an exception that allows someone to use a copyrighted work without permission.

Many people believe that the doctrine of copyright exploitation protects their right to use copyrighted material from third parties, as long as they behave fairly and do not, for example, sell pirated copies.

Suppose you find that your trademark's copyright material is being used unlawfully on social media channels. In that case, the first step is to contact the infringer. If you have any questions about your copyright or trademark, please contact your lawyer, who can advise you.

Simply paying tribute to the author of the original work is not always enough to avoid copyright infringement. Social media users should not assume that they have rewarded the work, perhaps by linking to a website. Make sure you do not infringe any trademark when you republish third-party content, as the original creators of that content may be able to assert trademark or copyright claims against your trademark. If you wish to obtain permission to use any of your rights, make sure you obtain written permission from the copyright holder.

Every social media platform you use has its own rules for images and copyrights, so you should check these rules before posting. When posting content on a social media platform, it is important to check whether you have the legal right to post such content and whether such posts could be liable for copyright infringement.

Regardless, most logos in the blog environment are probably fair use, so you have to be careful. The good news is that most blogs have no copyright or other issues. However, if you want to be especially safe, it would probably behoove you to go through the copyright process quarterly to mop up any stray ends and cover your content in that protective blanket.

Even if copyright is transferred to someone else, the design is yours only if all security measures are in place to protect against infringement and ensure that it does not infringe on other works' copyrights. Even if your logo were qualified, it is not copyrighted because it uses the word "copyright" in the title. Remember that!

If you do not make money from your website, content from others does not violate copyright. However, if you write to the author for permission, do not receive it, copy a protected work, and publish it on your blog, you have violated copyright and are subject to legal liability.

I know, I know, the world of copyright is extremely complicated. The take-home note here is always to be safe rather than sorry and never copy someone else's work.

www.ingramcontent.com/pod-product-compliance
Lightning Source LLC
Chambersburg PA
CBHW051236050326
40689CB00007B/946